· The Girlfriends' Clergy Companion ·

The Girlfriends' Clergy Companion

SURVIVING AND THRIVING IN MINISTRY

••••

Melissa Lynn DeRosia
Marianne J. Grano
Amy Morgan
Amanda Adams Riley

ALBAN

Herndon, Virginia
www.alban.org

The Alban Institute
2121 Cooperative Way, Suite 100
Herndon, VA 20171

Unless otherwise noted, all Scripture quotations are from the New Revised Standard Version of the Bible, copyright © 1989, Division of Christian Education of the National Council of the Churches of Christ in the United States of America, and are used by permission.

Cover Design by Signal Hill.

Library of Congress Cataloging-in-Publication Data

The girlfriends' clergy companion : surviving and thriving in ministry / Melissa Lynn DeRosia ... [et al.].
    p. cm.
  Includes bibliographical references (p. 163).
  ISBN 978-1-56699-418-7
  1. Women clergy--Conduct of life. 2. Young women--Conduct of life. I. DeRosia, Melissa Lynn.
  BV676.G55 2011
  253.082--dc23
                        2011017239

11   12   13   14   15   VP   5   4   3   2   1

Contents

••••

Foreword

. . . .

The receiver feels like it weighs fifty pounds when I place it onto its cradle. I exhale loudly. I was on the phone with the pastor who followed me at my last church. Thrilled that the congregation was doing so well after I left, I eagerly listened to stories of the current success. When I had left the congregation, I was careful to break my ties, but after loving people so achingly much for years, I found myself longing to hear the details of their lives and ministries.

My anticipation and excitement faltered when the pastor told me about a series of tough conversations he had had with the church leadership. As he told me about the necessary exchanges, my predecessor explained to me, "You were a *lot* nicer than I am." I laughed. From our conversation, it sounded like it was true. He was doing a great job at the church, partly because he had a wonderful way of being straight forward when I would have meandered. He knew how to be blunt, when I would have sugarcoated. Shortly after that comment, we ended the phone call.

The sigh leaves an empty space in my gut. I sense the growing pit in my stomach and I wonder what it could be. *I'm so happy for them. Why does this feel painful? Am I jealous?* I'm sure there is a tinge of envy tainting my complex emotions, but I know that's not all. I would be horrified if the church were doing poorly. I think hard about why this funk is settling upon me.

In my office, sorting out the details and my ensuing emotions, I remember the comment about my being nice. The pastor was not trying to put me down, not in any way. In fact, he was trying to be self-deprecating. But he further metastasized all those things that I had been told during the last dozen years of ministry, and they seem to multiply in my gut as I internalize them. I'm too sweet. I'm too emotional. I'm too sensitive. My skin is far too thin. I'm not strong enough.

Much of the criticism would have been the same for anyone entering the ministry. But, it somehow seems unfair for anyone to be saying these things about me. After all, I'm not all that sweet, emotional, sensitive, or weak. So I wonder if the comment had more to do with my petite frame and red lipstick than with my leadership style. From the professional feedback I receive, I imagine what a good pastor would look like, and a vision appears into my mind: it's a hammer with sociopath tendencies and the epidermis of an elephant.

Or does a good pastor look like something else? I hear a darker side within me whispering, seductively, *You know, you really wouldn't have these problems if you were a man.*

Inhaling the breath that I had just released, I realize that I'm not upset that the church is doing well. I'm concerned that I didn't do well enough. I worry that I'm not an adequate pastor because I once had to excuse my eight-month-pregnant self from the wedding rehearsal so that I could puke (why do they call it morning sickness when it can creep up on you on Friday night?). The mother-of-the-bride, who was steadfastly opposed to women clergy, heard me, outside of the stall. I was nervous she was going to ask if she needed to hold my hair back.

I never stayed for the postmeeting parking lot conversations, because I had to run home and nurse my baby, and I knew that I had to nurse my baby because. . . well. . . nursing moms, you can finish the rest of that sentence.

I constantly juggled my daughter on my hip as I prayed over the potlucks. I rarely had to remind myself to maintain a work–life balance, because the reminders of home were constantly tugging at my preaching robe, asking when we were going to leave.

I don't dare to pick up that fifty-pound office phone again. This time I reach for my earbuds, cell phone, and dial the number on my "favorites" list. The headphones feel weightless, and that pit that grew so rapidly in my belly begins to dissolve just as quickly, because I call a girlfriend. The sisterhood saves me from my despondency.

Sometimes just the sound of another woman in ministry reminds me of how crucial our role in our society is. That soothing moan lets me know that someone else shares the pain. Then I notice a gentle click, as her tongue registers the slightest bit of frustration on the roof of her mouth. When I get to the height of my complaints, I can almost hear her eyes rolling. Her comforting turns into mild disgust mingled with just a hint of cathartic cynicism. After that, we can move into that warm and beautiful laughter that seems to give me perspective and healing.

The voice of a friend, who knows the particular struggles and winsomeness of ministry, is a lifeline for me. I hang up, realizing that all the juggling, balancing, nurturing, and even some of the vomiting actively models leadership to a world that can be confused about the gifts and callings of women. Single women, female heads of household, spouses, lesbians, and mothers—we are working in the church, and as we do, we break down some of our culture's strongest gender barriers. Furthermore, we're doing it with style.

The book that you're holding in your hand or reading on your screen, this *Girlfriends' Clergy Companion*, is filled with those lifelines. It's a particular chorus of wise and funny women who don't talk down at us, but have the grace to walk alongside us, pointing out the pitfalls, laughing at the absurdities, and relishing the true joys of this momentous time in which God has called us to minister. If you are just starting out, or if you are seasoned in the art of pastoring, these girlfriends will tell you what you need to know, and they will make you feel less alone in your struggles. I'm thankful for these women who share their lives and experiences, reminding us of our peculiar and beguiling position, and giving us all those needed girlfriends.

CAROL HOWARD MERRITT

Preface

. . . .

My husband had no job. I had just weathered my first Michigan winter. I was in culture shock, trying to connect to Midwestern suburbanites. And the church I was serving was a mess. I needed girlfriends.

—Amy

I was taking a new call in the smallest town I had ever lived in. I was leaving a strong group of colleagues and friends. I knew there was one thing I needed, beyond God: other women with whom I could share my struggles and joys. I needed girlfriends.

—Amanda

I was serving my first call out of seminary as a solo pastor in a town where, I suddenly realized, I was the *only* female pastor. Exploring my regional governing body further, I learned that I was the only clergywoman under the age of fifty. It didn't take me long to realize that I needed girlfriends.

—MELISSA

I felt stranded in a suburban church and wasn't really sure what I was doing. I couldn't talk to young women in the real world, who only asked me questions about the Bible and requested prayers. I couldn't talk to other pastors about what to do with my hair. I needed girlfriends.

—MARIANNE

Who Are Girlfriends?

Girlfriends have no agenda.

Girlfriends are willing to talk with us about all our issues as they arise.

Girlfriends are able to share our triumphs, our difficulties, our ideas, and our dreams.

Each third Thursday of the month, a group of young women clergy become a group of girlfriends. We gather to eat, drink, and talk. We give thanks for what God is doing in our lives. We gain from one another's wisdom. Most important, we are able to understand that we are not alone, although we are a minority in this unique, challenging calling. Without this group of girlfriends, some of us would not have remained in the ministry.

We hear from other clergywomen that many of them *do* leave parish ministry. We would offer you statistics from our denomination (or others) if there were any to provide, but the studies focusing on women—never mind *young* women—in ministry are more than ten years old. We believe that a lot has changed in the past decade. As more and more young women begin the process of discerning a call to ministry, entering seminary, graduating, and searching for the call to a parish or other ministry setting, they need to be aware of the reality they face. The reality is that you may be the first woman pastor many people meet, and if not the first woman, the first woman who could be their child, sister, girlfriend, or grandchild. The truth is that we are a minority, and that fact alone can be isolating.

We believe that our regularly gathering for meetings and our fellowship could benefit others in this minority—young women—within a minority, clergy. We share our story, praying that you can gain from it. We came together through a vocational friendship grant, a program of the Lilly Foundation. The Rev. Amanda Adams Riley was completing the Lilly Endowment's Transitions into Ministry (TiM) program in Ann Arbor, Michigan, in the spring of 2007. She had accepted a call in a small town in the presbytery just north of the community where she had been serving. One thing she had learned from her time as a Lilly resident was the value of colleagues and the importance of receiving the support of other clergy. Knowing she would not have that advantage as the only clergywoman in the town and within a fifteen-mile radius of her new congregation, and knowing that close supportive relationships with male clergy can be awkward, especially for a single woman, she decided to start a group for young clergywomen in their first calls. Aware that there were close to a dozen young women in their first calls in her denomination serving in southeast and mid-Michigan, she collected e-mail addresses and called a meeting. One of the women graciously offered her home as a meeting place, and in August 2007 we had our first meeting. By October we had secured the vocational friendship grant from Lilly (made available to help clergy who have completed the residence program to make and maintain friendships), and we were on our way. While many women were unable to or declined to participate in the group, most of those who came to the first gathering continued to keep in touch through e-mail, even if they did not regularly attend the meetings. For those of us who made it every month, this group became a lifeline.

Friendships for clergy don't come easily. The few young people in our area with whom we might form friendships often have difficulty understanding who we are as "professionally religious" people and what we are doing in ministry. Unless you attended a Christian college and kept your head in the ground, the odds are that you know the reality: most people our age are not involved in church, and most cannot imagine what it means for someone their age to be ordained. Furthermore, our peers in other professions work different hours from those we do, making it hard for us to meet people. It's difficult to go out on Saturday night with friends when you know you have to bring your A-game to church on Sunday morning. Even those of us who serve on a church staff and have some built-in support recognize that there is something unique about the experience of being both young and a clergywoman.

After a year of meetings, our group spent a few days on retreat. During that time, we talked about the situation of young women clergy in our denomination and our concern for one another. We worshiped, read Scripture, shared communion, and prayed together. We dreamed, and we made commitments. One decision was to write to our denomination, the Presbyterian Church (U.S.A.), to request a clear, specific, denomination-wide policy for family leave. The other was to write this book.

The Girlfriends' Clergy Companion

Many of us have also found that through The Young Clergy Women Project (TYCWP), an effort to connect young women clergy online that began in 2006 with a grant from the Louisville Institute, we are beginning to form, rather than an "old boys' network," a "young girlfriends' network." We are able stay connected and to discuss common issues. We are able to share our reflections about ministry and life, particularly through the online magazine *Fidelia's Sisters*, a program of TYCWP. We felt a need, however, to model this online community as a face-to-face experience by helping other young clergywomen as they begin and continue in ministry, so we can all glorify God by being healthy and effective ministers.

Over and over at our meetings, we heard one another talking about what we wish we had known going into this calling. Over and over, we recognized that our experience as a group could be helpful to others. Those conversations grew into *The Girlfriends' Clergy Companion*. This book is not intended to help you develop your theology or understand the Bible. We assume you are doing that all the time, probably better than we are. This book is about the nitty-gritty—what you do with your hair, what it's really like to be a solo pastor, how to date, what to do when you're ready to quit.

We recognize that our experiences are limited, and that some of them may not apply to your situation. For one, none of us is part of a racial/ethnic minority. We see this as a reflection of the state of our denomination as a whole, and we chose not to seek someone out who had not been part of our group process. Likewise we lack an LGBT (lesbian, gay, bisexual, or transgendered) voice, and we see that fact also as a commentary on our denomination. We know that these voices are out there, and we see that there is more work to be done. Our book speaks from very particular experiences.

Yet we hope that by writing about our own situations, we will speak to young male clergy, young women clergy who are not Presbyterian, all clergy, and even the church at large. As young women clergy, we are a minority within the church. We are a new generation that is seeing the church with new eyes. Our hope is that we can see it accurately and describe it in ways that help the church to become more fully the city on a hill that Christ called it to be.

We will look at the church from several angles. Amy begins by discussing an experience seminaries don't often prepare their graduates to manage: the call process, or as we like to call it, "The Dating Game," and how young women clergy in particular can learn to navigate the ups and downs of finding a call. Next, we talk about the most common ministry situations in which young women find themselves in the church, either "Flying Solo," as described by Melissa, or finding yourself "The Eternal Associate," as Amy, Amanda, and Marianne are. Then, unlike typical resources for new clergy, this book addresses the fact that you are a human being and that your personal life will—surprise!—affect your ministry. We have included chapters on style, the single life, relationships, children, and self-care. In addition, we address the difficulties and challenges the church never tells you about in the chapters "Tiresome, Taxing, and Toxic: Difficult Situations in Ministry" and "When the Grass Looks Greener: Transitions in Ministry." The conclusion, "Treading Out the Grain: Remaining Faithful to the Call," reminds us all about the faithful work of ministry and shares where each one of us is today. We end each chapter with "The Girlfriend's Checklist," a practical summary of strategies you can use to be a more healthier and more effective minister.

God Calls Us to Be Girlfriends

When we discussed writing this book, we thought of one very young woman in ministry: Mary.

Mary received a call from God to perform a difficult, even life-threatening, task—to become pregnant out of wedlock and to deliver and raise a son who would be the savior of her people. When Mary received this call, she said yes. But immediately afterward, she traveled to visit another woman, her cousin Elizabeth. Elizabeth had her own calling, and she, too, was pregnant. In that visit, Mary was to gain strength from the wisdom of another woman who was a little farther along the road than she was, and the women would prophesy great things together. They were the first prophets of the New Testament age. If Mary needed strength, hope, and wisdom from someone in a similar calling, a girlfriend whom she could trust, why would we assume we have to do our ministry alone? We offer to be your Elizabeths. Come and visit with us.

Acknowledgments

This book came about as the result of a few days away from our churches, time spent in a house near Lake Michigan and funded by a Vocational Friendship Grant from the Lilly Endowment. The grant we received from Lilly funded eighteen months of lunches, a retreat, and child-care expenses once we began writing. We are indebted to the people at the Lilly Endowment for their willingness to try something new by giving grant money to clergy simply for the purpose of growing friendships. One result of the friendship we formed is this book.

We are all thankful for the support and encouragement of our congregations. Members and staff alike encouraged us as we took on this project, and while we are still growing and learning as pastors, we could not be who we are and know what we know without them.

We are thankful to the Alban Institute for taking a chance on a less-than-traditional book. We could not have gotten this all together without the help of the skilled staff at Alban who provided us with insight and encouragement along the way.

MELISSA

When we were in college and on our first date, I told Matthew, "I am going to be a minister. So if you aren't all right with that, we don't need a second date." The poor guy didn't know what he was getting into. I am grateful for his calm, constant, loving and supportive presence in my life. I am blessed by God's gift of community that has surrounded me on this journey in ministry. For my family—husband Matt; my life and light daughters, Lillian and Norah; and my mom, who has always told me that I am a gift from God—I love you. To the faithful community at the First Presbyterian Church, who with love, grace, and many cups of coffee taught me about ministry—thank you for your willingness to be open to the places where God was guiding and leading us.

MARIANNE

I give all the glory to Jesus, for "you have turned my mourning into dancing; you have taken off my sackcloth and clothed me with joy, so that my soul may praise you and not be silent" (Ps. 30:11–12). I am thankful to all the saints of God in my life, especially my husband and best friend, Dan; my little Froopster, Diana Mae; my loving and supportive parents, Garry and Sue; my mother-in-law, Maura; my brothers, brother-in-law, and sister-in-law; my grandparents, aunts, and uncles; and my girlfriends. I thank the saints of God at University Presbyterian Church, especially my colleagues in ministry, George, Carol, and Laura, and the dedicated servants of the Lord who work with the middle- and high-school youth groups and the confirmation class. To my church family: I love you all and thank you for the opportunity to be a part of your life. My efforts on this work are dedicated to the confirmation class and the middle- and high- school youth groups of UPC. Thank you for your energy and your questions, and for your many contributions to the Jesus Cup.

AMY

I praise our God who makes our dreams come true, even when we have not yet dreamt them. I feel so blessed to have a husband who loves me as I am and believes in me, who listens to me and gives me strength. I am thankful for my beautiful son and for his budding faith, which inspires me. I thank God for my parents, who planted the seed of faith in me and have always believed I can do anything I set my mind to, and for my Granny, who prayed for a pastor in the family and has prayed for me through my whole life. The congregation and staff at First Presbyterian Church of Birmingham have been caring and supportive, strong and wise. They have taught me so much, have been the body of Christ to me, and have celebrated my growth as a pastor and the dream come true of writing this book. I am grateful for my friends and colleagues in ministry who have encouraged my work on this book, especially the remarkable women who wrote it with me and helped me survive the challenges of my first years in ministry.

AMANDA

I am thankful to God for granting me the opportunity to begin my ministry in a call funded by the Lilly Endowment Transition into Ministry program, which taught me the value of colleagues in ministry and clergy friendships. I appreciate the help and support of all of my friends, especially the houseguests who became an unwitting part of the writing process. I am thankful for all of my mentors who have taught me so much about ministry and faith. I am who I am because of your example, guidance, and support. I am grateful to my husband, Bill, for his love and support during this experience, and to my parents, who taught me the faith I now hold so dear and who encouraged me in my call. This work would not have been possible without the support of the First Presbyterian Churches of Fenton and Ann Arbor, those beloved saints of God who taught me how to be a pastor, and the ongoing support of Brentwood Presbyterian Church, my new church home. And last but not least, I thank my girlfriends, without whom I would have never dared to take this adventure.

·1·

The Dating Game

A MATCH MADE IN HEAVEN FOR YOU AND THE CHURCH

Amy Morgan

• • • •

I love being a minister. Truly, I do. Yes, there are challenges and joys, pitfalls and privileges to being a pastor. But getting into the game is a trial and adventure all its own. How does a young woman get her foot in the door without "putting her foot in it"?

Accepting God's call to ministry can be a beautiful spiritual experience. We discern. We pray. We study. We work together, believing with all our hearts that the Holy Spirit will mystically intervene in our faithful adherence to church polity to bring about a happy and holy union between a congregation and a pastor.

But I can't say I felt the same way during the final three months of my seminary career. I had met all the necessary requirements to seek my first call to ordained ministry. But as the interview process with various churches lagged, cloaked in mystery and confidentiality, it hit me: I was about to *graduate*, and

I needed a J-O-B. Of course, the ministry of Word and Sacrament isn't a job, it's a *calling*. But when you're facing imminent expulsion from student housing, termination from your work-study job, and the prospect of living in your parents' basement for an indeterminate amount of time, suddenly you realize that what you need is not a calling but a *job*.

Maybe you're not in this situation. I hope the ordination process has been a breeze for you, and that you've felt God leading and guiding you through each step along the path. Perhaps you know just where you'll be heading postgraduation. You can frame your degree, the movers will show up a week later, and you'll be settled in your new home and new ministry without missing a pay period. If this is you, you're in the blessed minority. Godspeed, and you may skip the rest of this chapter. If, however, you are approaching or somewhere in the midst of the tempestuous process of becoming a pastor, read on for caution, advice, and hope.

Most church processes for entering ministry are at least somewhat bureaucratic, confusing, frustrating, or downright ridiculous. If you're in the Presbyterian call process, you're in the land of endless acronyms. You must meet with CPM, complete your required units of CPE, develop your PIF, interview with PNCs, and finally get your call approved by COM. Representatives from your denomination and board of pensions may provide workshops at your seminary about the call process and terms of call. I highly recommend that you attend these workshops and get your hands on as many resources as possible as you make your way through this maze. Whatever your denomination, make sure you understand the process, locate your resources, and identify as many helpful people as possible. Particularly if the seminary you attend is not associated with your denomination, you will need to take the initiative to acquire an adequate knowledge of next steps and resources to keep you out of the dreaded parental basement. (Full disclosure: the basement isn't so bad. I lived there for six months, and

I very gratefully survived until I received my first call.) Knowledge is power, baby.

Searching for a call, especially a *first* call, is somewhat akin to attempting to get picked for a kickball team. During your final months in seminary, you stand on the sidelines, watching as your classmates are offered this or that choice position, sometimes the very positions for which you interviewed brilliantly. You begin to wonder if, in fact, you are called to ministry. You wonder why no churches seem to agree with God on this matter, and panic begins to set in.

In many of the interviews for my first call, nominating committees seemed concerned that I would view the position at their church as a "stepping-stone." Some churches attribute an associate pastor's brief tenure to the pastor's professional ambition. My suspicion is that many young pastors are desperate for a *job* and will therefore assume that the Holy Spirit is at work in the first church to offer them a call. After months of searching, writing cover letters, making phone calls, and interviewing, one can become quite adept at rationalizing God's role in any call. Thus, we might be less than faithful in listening for God's voice in the call process, jump the gun, and end up in a toxic situation (more about this topic later in the book). Within two years, the toxicity of the call has become abundantly clear to us, our congregations, and anyone with ears who dares to approach us. Our first call may not be a "stepping stone" to bigger and better things. It may be more like a pothole we fall into and have to climb out of. It's little wonder that many pastors (male and female) find themselves wondering in their first five years of ministry if a career as a day trader isn't what God is really calling them to.

What it takes to survive this often grueling, soul-consuming process and to remain faithful in hearing God's call is humanity, humor, chutzpah, and a little TRUST: Talk, Rock, Understand, Study, Take. (I had to devise my own acronym. I am Presbyterian, after all.)

We're All Human, but You're a Woman

No matter how much you know, whom you know, or how smoothly your process goes, you will face frustrations along the way. And it's likely that at some point the process will frustrate you particularly because you are a woman. In all honesty, my male colleagues had plenty of troubles along the bumpy road to their first church. Statistically, however, it takes women longer to receive their first call, and they are paid less than their male counterparts in similar positions. Many of our frustrations are the same as those of any other person seeking to follow God's call to ministry in the church. Some of our challenges mimic those experienced by any young person today entering the secular workforce. Still, some aspects of being a young woman entering the ministry are unique.

Just as when you go out on a date for the first time, you might be looking for Prince Charming in your first call. Chances are, you won't find him. First, you don't really know what you're looking for. Unless you've worked in the church for years before entering ordained ministry, you don't really know what life is like under the robe until you've tried it on. Second, many of the "choice" positions will be filled by your male counterparts. While your male classmates may have their age and experience working against them as they strive for those big-steeple pulpits, you have an added strike against you: anatomy that doesn't match most churches' ideal for a shiny new pastor. One girlfriend's mentor told her that what every church is really looking for in a pastor is "Jesus with a young family." Sorry, ladies, but Jesus, though he was many things, was not a woman.

Those denominations that ordain women may require churches to interview women and minorities for any open position, but they don't require churches to change their traditional views or ideals. Those kinds of changes, unfortunately, just can't be made a requirement. As I often remind my parishioners, the church is made up of human beings. People in the church are stunningly similar to people outside the church.

We have stereotypes and fallen understandings about human relationships, and we miss God's kingdom vision. Changes in perspective are coming with time and experience, but they're not here yet. As a woman in ministry, you'll have to learn to work with the church as it is so that you can then work to make it what it ought to be.

Have a Plan Q

As I was approaching graduation, I thought I had *the* perfect call in the bag. It was everything I thought I was called to do and be, and it was in the perfect location. I continued interviewing with other churches—just as a backup, you know. My anxiety level, however, began to creep up when, after graduation, the call process continued to drag on, and I had not yet been extended a call to any church. I was one of two final candidates for two calls. I was feeling pretty good. Odds were, I'd have a *job* in a few weeks. I had a Plan A and a Plan B. Who could ask for more? Imagine the crushing sense of defeat and total horror when I was not offered either call. My husband had already left his job, our contract with seminary housing would end in a few weeks, and we had a five-month-old baby. We really needed to be prepared for anything on the wild and unpredictable roller coaster that is the movement of the Spirit. We lived with my parents for six months and eventually landed where God wanted us, but that wild and terrifying ride certainly was not what I had imagined as the culmination of my seminary training.

As you creep ever nearer to becoming a basement dweller, you will undoubtedly try your best to remain faithful to your sense of God's call on your life. But we all have to pay the bills, secure health-insurance coverage, and find a stable home. The hope I can offer you is this: even after all my trials and tribulations, I still believe the Holy Spirit is driving this crazy train—which means that you have to figure out how to pack for the ride. For some, that might be easy. Just pack light and keep that hopeful and adventurous spirit. For type-A personalities like me, you might need a very large suitcase. First, you will want to prepare for the worst-case scenario. Figure out how you're going to get by for at least a year without a call—how you're going to get health insurance, what you'll do for work, whose basement you'll move into (we actually had three offers). Have all that in place before you even start looking. Go into the call process with confidence that you don't have to find a *job*. But get a job, if necessary. Then find your calling. It's an enormous letdown, after three years of seminary, to go back to an ordinary job. You are all set to get out there and be "the Reverend" and change the world. However, it's a much bigger letdown to discover that your first "call" is actually just a job, because you were too poor, uninsured, and emotionally drained to start another round of interviews.

Learn How to Interview

Interviewing for a call to ministry is not the time to display how virtuously humble you are. Nor is it a time to hop in the back seat and let someone else drive. God is partnering with you in this process, and you've got to step up and do your part. Early in the interview process, I had the sense that the Holy Spirit was just going to drop the ideal ministry in my lap. All I had to do was show up for interviews on time, and God would take care of the rest. I had some very poor first interviews. Eventually, I learned that I had to be prepared to interview well, ask good questions, and take responsibility for my part in the call process.

Every church will ask what you think your strengths and weaknesses are. Just as you would in the "real" world, you highlight your strengths and explain how your weaknesses really are strengths in the end. And you say it as though you just discovered that fact in the moment, and the pastoral search committee has done a good deed in boosting your self-esteem. Many young women (and young men) entering ministry don't have a strong human resources background or a ton of interviewing experience under their belt. My advice to you: *get some.* There's plenty of good interviewing advice online at any job-search site if you happen to be lacking friends in the human resources department. Practice interviewing with friends. Call church members you know who have served on search committees, and ask them to try to remember the kinds of questions they asked.

Speaking of Questions . . .

In my first meeting to begin the ordination process, I was asked by a member of my church session (governing board), "So what are you going to do about having children?" I was newly married and entering seminary, and while it was certainly none of these people's business what I was going to do about having children, I didn't have the good sense to keep my personal life personal. I told the dozen or so people gathered there that I thought it was completely insane for anyone to try to have children while in seminary. My son was born three weeks before the start of my last semester. Never say never. And never answer questions that shouldn't be asked in the first place.

But the real moral of this story is that, as a woman in the church, you will almost certainly be asked questions that should never be asked. People in the church, I've found, can pose profoundly inappropriate and even illegal questions to candidates for employment and ministry.[1] While this pitfall is disappointing no matter what your age or gender, young women can expect to be asked questions that will not be asked of your male (or your older female) counterparts.

While my denomination, like several others, has been ordaining women to ministry for a good half-century now, the prospect of a woman in the pulpit is still unnerving for many. Many congregations have never had a female pastor. Many more have never had a woman as a head of staff. While it might be easy to see a male pastor as that preacher/theologian-in-residence that seminary prepares us to be, when a woman is being considered, many congregations aren't sure what they should expect.

In the numerous interviews most of us must undergo to receive a call, many will begin with the standard, agreed-upon set of questions. But watch out for follow-ups, questions that begin with, "I see here that you wrote . . . ," and anything that follows the words, "Does anyone have anything else they'd like to ask?" Yes, these are standard parts of the interview, but this is the point in the interview at which inappropriate questions are most often inserted. This is when you can expect such questions as, "Will your husband attend church here?" "What is your opinion of dating church members?" "When do you expect to start having children?" "Do you think you'll get married?" "Do you have a problem with God the Father?" and statements like "If you don't bring in new members, we're sure that you can breed them in." Truth is stranger than fiction. I've had male clergy friends who were asked whether their wife would be singing in the choir and others who were told they would certainly draw younger women into the church. We'll deal more extensively in later chapters with managing your personal relationships in ministry. The point here is to be prepared for those questions that should never be asked and comments that should never be made.

You may really love a church, and you may feel called to ministry there. You may connect to the members of the search committee immediately. And then someone will ask or say something that is patently offensive or idiotic. Now you have to decide how to handle this. Do you not take the call, assuming this person is expressing the attitudes of the whole church? Do you dismiss the comment, assuming this is the viewpoint of one ignorant (or possibly just nervous) member?

While it's up to you to decide, my advice to you is this: don't let offensive remarks go unnoticed, but don't let them cloud your judgment. Ask a follow-up question to gauge how the other members of the committee are reacting. You'll be able to tell fairly quickly from the red faces or heavy sighs if the rest of the committee is embarrassed by the question or remark. If you're not getting a good reading, and you have to assume the question has not been asked of your male counterparts, you may need to be more direct. Ask why the information the member has asked for is important to the committee. While it would be nice to be able to tell people that the question they have asked is too personal, you are interviewing for a pastoral position in which you will be privileged to personal information about your church members. It may seem natural for them to want to have a good deal of personal information about you. Especially if the church has not previously experienced a female pastor, the inappropriate and personal questions may be expressing the parishioners' need for you to paint a picture for them of what they can expect of your ministry.

These are hard questions to address head-on, but if you don't do it now, it will smack you in the back of the head later. If the committee as a whole is embarrassed by one member's question or remark, the others likely won't come to your aid. You may or may not be offered or accept this call, but they have to keep being in Christian community, and, more important, serve on this search committee with the offensive question-asker for an indeterminate amount of time. While they may not defend you, they do want to see you handle the situation pastorally and, perhaps even more important, authoritatively. I've witnessed a number of pithy-yet-respectful comebacks to inappropriate questions asked of female pastoral candidates. But you have to have your head in the game, keep your cool, and take all the time you need to respond.

Don't Let Elephants Sit in the Room

If something feels uncomfortable, say so. To make a gross generalization, women pick up on tension or high emotion in a room much more quickly and accurately than men. Use this sensory aptitude to your advantage, and don't let the tension be one more factor that makes an interview miserable. A simple, "It feels as though there is a lot of tension in the room. Is there something going on that you want to tell me about?" will suffice. You may find out that the head of staff is pressuring the committee to make a decision quickly. You may discover that some major upheaval is going on in the church that might influence your sense of call (in one direction or another). There might be some major disagreement within the committee about your fitness for ministry. Whatever you learn, it will be helpful information for you, and the committee will be more at ease knowing the elephant has moved on to greener jungles.

God Has a Sense of Humor— So Should You

Your ideal call may not look anything like what God has in store for you. Be open to looking outside your desired geographical area and ministry specialty. I hope you have developed your own sense of what a call to ministry is about, but part of that sense should take into account the fact that God, not you, is in control of this process. Be yourself—the wonderful woman made in God's image that you are—as you go through the call process. It is difficult to hear and discern the right call in an environment with a lot of stress and noise. In the call process, everyone is nervous, anxious, and fearful. The committees are worried about finding the *right* pastor, and you are worried about making sure you go where God sends you *and* that your bills get paid next month. There's nothing you can do about search committees. But you can keep your own sense of humor intact. Take a bit of the seriousness and anxiety out of the situation, and you'll be doing everyone a huge favor, including God.

I'm sure you know the difference between appropriate and inappropriate humor. OK—I *hope* you do. I'm giving you the benefit of the doubt. But plenty of people don't know how to distinguish between what's funny in one situation and what's offensive in another. I had one girlfriend who found herself interviewing with a regional board of ministers for a position. Much of the meeting was spent listening to crude, demeaning, sexist jokes told by members of the all-male board. These were *pastors*, possible future colleagues! She, of course, couldn't join in the fun, and she was shocked and baffled by the situation. I hope you'll never have to experience such extreme circumstances, but be prepared to handle inappropriate humor. Don't pretend something is funny when it's not.

Be sensitive to how you are using humor as well. When interviewing for a youth pastor position, you might be tempted to throw in a "That's what *she* said" to show how well you can relate to middle-school boys. Not a good plan. Humor is great for lightening the mood, helping people feel comfortable in an anxious situation. But be sure the joke isn't made at another's expense and is not demeaning to any category of people (which pretty much rules out *all* middle-school-boy humor).

TRUST: Talk, Rock, Understand, Study, Take

Talk to the committee, talk to references, talk to anyone who knows anything about the church. Talk to friends who are interviewing at the same churches you are to see whether they got similar impressions about the church (you don't have to ask them how they answered the interview questions or if the committee smiled at them more). Talk to friends from the area where you're interviewing. Talk to people to gather information, to discern your thoughts and feelings about the churches you're considering, and to hear God speaking to you through their voices.

Rock the interview. "Rocking" an interview means participating in faithful dialogue, not selling yourself. Be yourself. Be the pastor God is calling you to be, even though you may have no idea yet what that will mean. You do need to be your very best self, but you don't need to be the self anyone else wants you to be.

A good interview doesn't mean that the committee loved you and wants to issue a call tomorrow. I once had a spectacular interview with a church that thought very differently than I do on a particular theological point. One committee member really liked me and was trying to persuade the rest of the committee that I was "the one." But it was obvious to me that the rest of the committee had been convinced by the head pastor that this one issue was the most important factor in calling a pastor to this church. I knew this going into the interview, and I had a wonderful, faith-filled discussion with the committee members. We both knew from the start that I wouldn't be called there, but I was grateful for the opportunity to articulate my position and express my hopes and blessings for their future ministry. Likewise, they were very gracious in their speaking and listening.

Understand what you and the church really want. It can be difficult to get clarity about what a church is looking for. In my denomination, churches have to fill out an information form explaining in detail who they are as a congregation and what they're looking for. But these forms can be full of coded or loaded language that you may not be able to decipher. Take whatever information you're given, and ask lots of pointed questions to gain clarity. How many hours a week will you be expected to work? How much of that time do the members want you to spend in the office? What kinds of expectations do they have about your personal life? Many churches express a desire for their pastors to have a "strong relationship with Jesus Christ" or a "visible and steadfast faith walk." How will they determine this about you? How will they judge whether your ministry is successful? Are the expectations they have of the pastor the same expectations they had for their male pastor in the 1950s who had 2.5 children and a wife at home to keep everything spotless, bake brownies, and sing in the choir?

I had one mentor who served a church for many years as a single woman. She later married and had a child. While the church rejoiced over her marriage and embraced her child, some resented the fact that she wasn't always available since she now also had to pick her child up from preschool and attend her child's various activities (which were not extensive). The congregation had come to expect that they could have this pastor's full attention. When she became a wife and a mother, she was just as excellent a pastor. But members' perception was that she was no longer the pastor they had called. Interestingly enough, when this pastor left the congregation, the next pastor called was a single woman.

It's also important that you be clear about your expectations. One pastor I know sets a limit of working two evenings a week. I've yet to be able to set such boundaries, but if you're able to come to this kind of understanding up front, it will serve you well, especially when you have children who would like you to tuck them in at night on occasion. Make sure the church understands how you see your role in ministry. If you have no intention of riding in on a white horse and saving the congregation, make that as clear as possible. If you expect that your days off will be your days off, let the church know that up front.

You will likely still encounter surprises in your ministry, even if you set up clear expectations in the interview. My first call was supposed to be 95 percent youth ministry. The committee truly believed that was what I'd be doing because I was replacing a nonordained youth director. However, I knew the dynamic would be somewhat altered by the fact that the church was losing its head of staff. I couldn't have imagined at that time that three years later I would be the church's only associate pastor. I still minister with youth, but my responsibilities are very different from what was outlined in the interview. I'm loving it now, but the transition was bumpy.

Try your best to understand what you and the church really want and expect, and communicate clearly through the interviews, but be prepared to deal with surprising developments.

Study the church. Ask for information (budgets, finance reports, mission studies) from the churches you are seriously considering. Check out their websites (assuming—hoping—that they *have* websites) and read everything on them. Ask the committee about the church's history, previous pastors (particularly those in the position you are interviewing for), traditions, and prominent members. Find out how the community surrounding the church views this congregation. A question I asked at every interview was, "What is the 'word on the street' about this church?" Follow up by asking other pastors in the area or regional church leaders for their impression of the church. Does the church advertise in the local papers? What sorts of community events does the church sponsor, host, or participate in? Asking for this much information may sound invasive, I know, and the committee might take offense if you ask for it in a less-than-sensitive manner, but this is essential data for your study of a church.

Find out as much as you can about the community. You will thereby gain not only important information about where you will potentially be living, but also a clue as to how in tune the church is with the community in which it is located. Perhaps the church prides itself on its diversity. If you then discover that the community surrounding it is relatively homogeneous, you might ask what members mean when they talk about diversity. If the church claims solidarity with the poor but is located in a wealthy suburb, find out how members see themselves living out that solidarity. If you discover a thriving arts community around the church but see no sign of a flourishing arts ministry within the church, that discrepancy might raise questions for you.

Study this church and its surroundings the way you would research your finest exegetical work. Remember, this is not just a job. It's a place where you're going to live and minister for, God willing, a significant length of time. Few pastors get to move to familiar surroundings in their first call, so do your homework on your potential new home.

Take the call (if God tells you to). OK, this one sounds a little obvious, but the call of God is not always easy to discern. It's also important to realize that you are an active participant in this process. You may be offered a call at a time when you are still interviewing with other churches. You may be fortunate enough to be offered two or more calls that you must choose from. Or you may have searched for months and finally receive an offer, but feel unsure whether you are really called to that ministry. This can be one of the most agonizing parts of the call process and requires a lot of prayer and soul-searching. This is the time to ask questions you may not have considered earlier.

- Will my gifts and skills (as I understand them) be appreciated and useful in ministry in this place?
- Where might God be calling me to grow as a pastor and person, and how might this call contribute to that growth?
- Will I be able to minister effectively here on a personal level?
- Do I feel the pull of the Holy Spirit in some meaningful way to this place?

You'll need to clear away the clutter of needing a J-O-B, wanting to live in a particular locale, envisioning yourself in a certain kind of life, and open up your imagination to let God work on giving you a vision for your future ministry.

Once you've discerned that a particular church is truly where God is calling you (and the search committee has gotten a similar divine message), you're ready to accept a call. But taking the call is not quite as simple as saying "Here am I, Lord. Send me." You now have to put on your big-girl panties and negotiate the terms of your employment with the church, and once again, you need to do your homework. In my denomination, the salaries of all pastors are public information. Other denominations publish salary guidelines based on the size of the congregation, the pastor's role, and other factors. If such information is available to you, use it! Find out what churches of similar size in your area are paying pastors in your position with similar experience. Two years after taking my first call, I learned from a male friend of mine in a smaller church in my area that because he had checked out my salary before he negotiated his terms, he had asked for more money (and got it)! A girlfriend who served on a committee overseeing the terms negotiated by pastors in her area was shocked to discover what some people will ask for (and get). It's not just about money. Most denominations have some minimum standards, but such benefits as vacation and study leave, sabbatical, housing, office space, book allowances, travel allowances, and even maternity leave are all up for negotiation. I've heard of pastors asking for cell phones (with the calling plan paid for, of course), laptop computers, and even administrative support.

Now at this point, I hope you're saying to yourself, "But this is the church! This is not the place for self-advancement and greed!" Your indignation is duly noted. And I agree that, in some cases, your indignation is warranted. I would also caution you not to negotiate your way out of a position to which you feel deeply called. However, you also don't want to settle for less than you can live on (or live with). If the walls of the office you will be inhabiting sixty hours a week are painted puce, and that happens not to be your favorite color, it really isn't a bad idea to address this preference up front. Do it before you discover that the church refuses to repaint the office because it was just repainted to get it ready for the new pastor or because the growth chart of the former pastor's beloved child is marked on the wall in permanent ink.

Something like a laptop might seem extravagant until you discover that all the church plans to provide for you is a 1966 Olympia "DeLuxe" typewriter. Unless you were blessed with enough graduation cash to set up your own twenty-first-century office, you might want to think about helping the church make the millennial leap.

Another shocker: most churches have a small enough staff that they don't have to comply with the federal Family Medical Leave Act. While many churches are compassionate and thrilled to have you bring a new life into their midst, many will struggle with how to work out maternity leave. Save yourself the tension and heartache: even if you have no imminent plan of childbearing, discuss maternity leave (and any other medical leave you think might be necessary for you and your family) in your original terms.

When it comes down to final decision making, people like to say, "It's not about the money." Well, as I was told by one search committee, it's always about the money. The advice I was given was to work out your personal budget (keeping in mind the cost of living in your new community)[2], and decide what you will need to live on—not today but in five years. Because many pastors don't receive even cost-of-living raises, if you ask for what you can live with for five years, you can remain in your position for at least that long. After that point, you have to decide if you can ask for more (if you need it) or if it's time to move on. The last thing you want to do is to begin your ministry broke and then get even more broke because you didn't negotiate for what you truly needed. If the church to which you feel called is not in a financial position to offer you what you need, there are options for you and for them. For clergy, salary is subject to both income tax and Social Security and Medicare taxes, housing allowance is subject only to Social Security and Medicare taxes, and some other allowances are tax exempt. Some money is counted when calculating pension payments; some isn't. If you can live with a smaller cash salary (perhaps because you have a spouse with a decent job), you can make more with less by asking for more in housing and other tax-exempt allowances. And there are some things money can't buy. My church wasn't able to give me a raise for several years, but my son has been allowed to attend the church's weekday programs free of charge. Over the years, our family has enjoyed thousands of dollars of excellent child care and preschool I would have had to pay for. Creative negotiating works out for everyone.

The Higher Power

When I was in seminary, many people asked me if I would seek a call in Michigan, because that is where my husband's family lives. I informed them that it would be a warm day in Michigan before I moved to that icy wasteland. Many people also somehow sensed that I would go into youth ministry. Funny, because I never expressed the slightest interest in it. But it seems churches that might squirm at a woman in the pulpit will sometimes consent to a woman playing guitar around a campfire. I informed those who encouraged me toward youth ministry that I don't play the guitar.

Today, of course, I am a youth pastor in Michigan. It's the only proof I have that the call process is indeed completely directed by a higher power. It hasn't always been dreamy, but it is undoubtedly where God has called me to be. So take heart and have faith, my girlfriends. God has a mate in mind for you. Just be ready to play the game.

The Girlfriends' Checklist

* No one is perfect; you probably won't find your Prince Charming on the first date.
* Have a Plan Q.

- Learn to interview well.
- Don't let elephants sit in the room. If you sense there may be something the call committee is not telling you, find out what it is.
- Be prepared for inappropriate comments and humor.
- Remember to TRUST God and:
  - *Talk* to anyone who knows anything about the church.
  - *Rock* the interview.
  - *Understand* what you want and what the church wants.
  - *Study* the church.
  - *Take* the call (and negotiate well)!

·2·

Flying Solo

BEING *THE* WOMAN PASTOR

Melissa Lynn DeRosia

• • • •

T he church was overwhelmingly beautiful. Light streaming through stained-glass windows flooded the sanctuary with rainbows. The steeple stood prominently at the front of the building, with a bell ringing out over the downtown of the village. The search committee boasted that First Presbyterian was the only "downtown church" that had a working bell tower.

The building held the memories and stories of generations of churchgoers in this small Midwestern town. In every room you could smell Church—stale coffee, mildew, crayons, and a mixture of aftershave and old-lady perfume. I secretly believe that this is what God smells like. The mauve carpet had seen the spills of one too many potlucks. Now-tarnished brass nameplates "in memory of" were affixed to everything that wasn't nailed down.

The search committee and I were in conversation about our call—my call to be their pastor and their call to take a chance on a young, fresh-from-seminary, female pastor. We were all giddy and naively optimistic about the journey God was laying out before us.

Then I saw it.

The wall.

The wall is in the church parlor, where people gather after service to drink coffee and catch up on the town news, and it can be seen from the sanctuary when a curtain is opened to accommodate the rare overflow crowd. On this wall are mounted, from floor to ceiling, photographs of every pastor who has served the church for more than one hundred years. As I scanned the wall, I quickly noticed: all of the pastors were male—and all of them were staring at me.

I stood there staring back at them in disbelief that I might be the first woman whose portrait would someday hang on this wall. I grew up in a church that always had a woman pastor. I went to a seminary where more than half the students were women. How was it possible that I would be the first woman pastor whose portrait hung on this wall?

It was possible, although some people from the congregation told the pastoral search committee, "If you ever call a woman pastor, I won't come to church anymore." It was possible, even though in this town, where there were more churches than restaurants and hair salons combined, there wasn't one female pastor to be found. My feelings of disbelief evolved into wondering why I would want a call to be *the* first woman solo pastor of this congregation to become reality.

Falling into Flight

As I searched for a new call, I felt as though I was being pushed out of the nest of higher education that had protected me from having too many "real life" experiences in ministry. I took one year off after college and brushed up on my coffee-shop barista skills before I went to seminary, because an internship in a congregation didn't offer health-care insurance or a livable wage. In seminary, my time was filled with classes, homework, and only short-term internships. When I graduated, these experiences left me feeling that I didn't know the first thing about what kind of position in ministry I was searching for.

True, I did not have a wealth of ministry experiences in my back pocket, but no graduating seminary student has many options. Most churches that are willing to consider a pastor with no experience are searching for a solo or associate pastor. Without a clue as to what kind of position would be a good fit for me, I simply hoped and prayed that I would "fall into" the call that God wanted me to be in. Practically speaking, that meant that in the initial stages of my search for a first call, I applied for a variety of positions.

As I started interviewing with search committees, I began to notice the kinds of questions the committees asked me and how I responded:

"In what ways will your gifts strengthen our youth program?"

"Our senior pastor is an excellent preacher, so will it be all right if you preach only six or eight times a year?"

"How will you encourage participation in our small-group ministry?"

I really didn't feel called to youth ministry. I love to preach, so, no, it wouldn't be all right if I preached only a couple times of year. I didn't have a clue as to what "small-group ministry" even meant.

As excited as I was about the possibility of working with other colleagues in ministry and focusing my gifts in a few specific areas like mission or congregational care, there were aspects of serving as an associate pastor that I didn't feel called to. Each time I hung up the phone after an initial interview, I couldn't shake the feeling of disappointment that I wouldn't be preaching more than once a month. I didn't want to spend my time in just one area of ministry; I wanted to try a little bit of everything. Even though at the start of my search process, I thought I would fall into the ministry where God wanted me, I ended up flying with confidence that God was calling me to serve as a solo pastor. I realized that I was called to preach, plan creative worship experiences, provide pastoral care, develop intergenerational education programs, partner in ministry with those on the margins of society, and discern with a congregation as we listened to God and one another for ways to be the body of Christ in the world today.

Is the Pastor Here?

When I landed as the first female pastor of this congregation, I spent a lot of my time in my office with the door open, getting to know the people of the church and the community. From time to time, someone trying to sell church photo directories or wanting to put up a poster to advertise a community concert would arrive at my door and ask:

"Is the pastor here?"

"I am the pastor."

"Are you the youth pastor?"

"No. I'm *the* pastor."

"Just you?"

"Just me."

"Huh."

The person standing at my office door would shift uncomfortably, look away, and hand me whatever literature he or she was passing out. The first couple of times this happened, I clenched my fists to keep the outrage I felt from escaping. The tone of the visitor's response expressed skepticism about my call, ordination, and ability to lead a congregation because I am not a man. The questioning tone of voice was mixed with wonder and confusion, but mostly people seemed to dismiss the possibility that a woman would ever be able to do a job that a man "should" do.

I didn't know what to do with the assumption that I must be the church secretary. I grew up in a congregation that didn't challenge my call to ministry because of my gender. In fact, the church I attended through my childhood always included a female clergyperson on staff. I watched a woman preach sermons, baptize, and lead the liturgy of communion with elements in hand. I pursued ministry in the denomination in which I was raised, in part because of my understanding that the way for women to be ministers was clear.

It wasn't until college, during a Bible study sponsored by a nondenominational megachurch, that a student, a member of the church, challenged me, saying, "You can't be a minister— you're a woman." With Bible open and finger pointing to Paul's first letter to Timothy, he explained that women did not have the authority to teach men and speak publicly in worship. If I wanted to serve God and the church, I could teach Sunday school to small children or be a secretary. I defended God's call for me and all women who felt called to serve in ministry, engaging in conversations with voices of opposition when I faced sexism in college *and* when it showed up again at my doorstep.

Standing there with the church-directory salesperson and the doubting voice, I flashed back on all the voices I had heard from college to the present that had challenged my call to ministry because of my gender. After I explained that I was indeed *the* pastor, the visitor would treat me that way. For the next fifteen minutes, I stood there like a pastor, listening to the sales pitch, to the explanation that all members of the congregation who had their photo taken for the directory would receive a free five-by-seven portrait.

It wasn't just the photo-directory salespeople and conservative students from a college Bible study who challenged my call to serve as *the* woman pastor of a congregation. There was some skepticism among the congregation's own members. It didn't take long to figure out who had been muttering and whispering about my being a woman and *the* pastor. I was surprised to discover, however, that most of the individuals in the congregation who had the most trouble with a female pastor in the pulpit were women. I had been warned about this possibility by

a wise pastor-mentor from seminary, but at the time I couldn't
envision it. In my mind, women in a congregation would be especially supportive and excited to see a woman in a position of
power and leadership. What I learned was that some women re-
sent seeing another woman fulfill a calling that they were never
even given the option to pursue. They may have felt a calling
to ministry or another form of church leadership and were denied the option, because at that time women weren't allowed to
be ordained, or they believed the message that women's roles
at church were confined to caring for children, cooking meals,
and attending to secretarial tasks. Now, here before them was
a woman who stood for all that they had hoped for, longed for,
were called to, and were denied.

I didn't always know why some members of the congregation or community struggled with and others openly welcomed
my being *the* woman pastor. I did know that almost everyone
had a story about their experiences with previous pastors, the
church, and their faith. Aside from preaching, what I felt particularly drawn to in solo ministry was the opportunity to hear
and engage the stories of individuals in the congregation. I felt
called to create space where these stories could be told and to
be open to how these stories, along with the stories of the Bible,
could guide and shape who God is calling us to be as a community of faith. As much as I wanted to push away the feelings of
resentment by the women of the congregation and rejection by
the men, I challenged myself to find ways to help people share
their stories about their lives, the life of the congregation, and
how God was speaking to us today.

One Cup at a Time

I was a solo pastor. Finding ways for people to share their stories
wasn't about investing a lot of time researching the best curriculum or purchasing supplies. I relied on something that already
flowed freely and found its way into nearly every gathering of

the church. Coffee. The large percolator coffee pot was started before worship every Sunday. During silent pauses of a prayer, we could hear the pot entering its final stages of brewing. After the benediction and handshakes, the worshipers moved from the sanctuary to the parlor, where they filled their cups and shared with one another the stories of their week.

As we gathered around tables, I saw arthritic fingers being warmed by the cup they held and young children dropping cookie crumbs on the floor. People shared stories about health concerns, school plays, new grandbabies, and what business was coming or going from the downtown main street. Sitting at those tables, I quickly learned that one of the most powerful aspects of ministry for a solo pastor of a small congregation was the gift of sipping a cup of coffee after worship and listening to stories about the places where faith intersects with everyday life.

Coffee became a catalyst for these after-worship gatherings, and they soon started happening during the week. On Thursday morning, I would start up a pot of coffee, and church members would stop in between doctor appointments or before running their next errand to see how everyone was doing. A faithful group of folks came every week, and others stopped in as their schedules allowed. It was here that I listened to the stories about the church. I heard about "the good old days" when church membership and attendance were at their peak— when there was a youth group, and so many kids in Sunday school that there wasn't enough meeting space in the building. The members of the congregation told stories about the pastors whose pictures were affixed to the parlor wall and the ways their leaders shepherded the church through change. The stories were told in a variety of ways, all expressing the pain the congregation went through as economic downturn and population decreases in the county meant that people from the church were losing jobs and moving away, and young people weren't coming back.

It was with a cup of coffee in hand that we talked about how much the church, this town, and the world were changing. My being there as a young woman pastor represented just how much their church had changed in the past fifty years, and in the safety of the church parlor, members were willing to bring out into the open what those changes were. The perceptions of those changes weren't always positive, but I was encouraged by the way the congregants shared their stories and how the experiences of the past and present were moving us into God's future for the church.

Beginning from this foundation—being able to openly share our stories in conversation over a cup of coffee, I drew on resources about Appreciative Inquiry[1] to formulate questions about congregational identity and the moments in all those stories when people celebrated the best of who they were and who they could be. Members of the congregation expressed how with a male pastor they felt that an agenda was being pushed from "the top down." With a woman in leadership implementing a conversational approach to ministry, they sensed a partnership between all the members of the church and the pastor.

The Church Secretary Can Preach

The ministry that happened over coffee also empowered me to embrace my own identity as *the* woman pastor. Of course, all sorts of stereotypes and assumptions were at work—that as a woman I would be better at washing the dishes than mowing a lawn, and as a woman pastor I would be better at educating children than running a meeting. As *the* woman solo pastor, however, I found that there was very little in the life of the church that I wasn't involved in. There wasn't a head of staff to turn to for insight on the church budget. No beloved associate pastor who visited the shut-ins and made hospital calls. No Christian educator to choose curriculum and organize Sunday school teachers. No sexton to unlock the building when the

AA group forgot its key (again). In fact, there wasn't even a secretary to fold the bulletins. There was me.

This was my first call, and I had nothing to compare it to. I didn't necessarily know what I was supposed to do, and I made missteps in my first couple of years. No one asked me to push the mower around the church lawn when a volunteer forgot to show up. But after the church secretary quit and the board of elders decided not to replace her, I became the paid "church lady" who typed everything, made the copies, answered the phone, helped prepare and clean up after meals, *and* put together a sermon, offered educational opportunities, and provided pastoral care. To a congregation with a struggling budget, such an arrangement can seem like a financial dream come true, but eventually, as the overworked, underpaid pastor, I began asking myself why I had bothered to go to seminary to learn how to print address labels.

I can imagine that this kind of scenario *could* happen to a man serving as a solo pastor in a small congregation. But I can't help but wonder if the elimination of paid administrative support in a congregation comes as easily when a man is serving as pastor. Are these conversations—about who will assume administrative duties when there is no longer money in the budget for a paid staff person—shaped by gender stereotypes? Is it "easier" for a congregation not to pay for a secretary when the pastor is a woman because they take for granted that she will "naturally" take on making copies and answering the church phone?

I wish I had had the experience in ministry to ask myself those questions and to be better prepared for setting good boundaries and making sure that while I was "flying solo," I wasn't going it alone as the church secretary who could preach. Looking back, I would have made sure I had a job description and that it was reviewed at least annually with the session. There was a job description used to explain what the pastor nominating committee was looking for in a pastor when it was conducting the search. It vaguely described the role of a pastor, which included preaching, teaching, and providing pastoral care. I failed to review and ask clarifying questions about the committee's expectations of my time and energy in "performing administrative duties," and in relationship to other responsibilities like preaching and teaching.

Girl Power

The good news about these experiences in ministry as a solo pastor is that these kinds of conversation can happen fairly easily if you talk with the board of elders or a few people designated to act as a "personnel committee." Even though I didn't ask these questions, I did pull together that group of folks who had served as a search committee for monthly "check-ins" about how things were going and what kind of feedback they were hearing from the congregation. Since they were no longer the pastor nominating committee—because Presbyterians love to use acronyms, the PNC—they decided that they needed a new name and acronym. The group understood its purpose to be one of support and mentoring and aptly identified itself as the pastor mentoring and support committee, or the PMS committee. We laughed every month when the calendar in the bulletin read "PMS Committee Meeting, 7:00 p.m."

One piece of feedback this group offered was to debrief a situation that happened at a meeting of church elders where I served as moderator. One of the elders expressed a heartfelt desire for me to "take charge of the situation and just start telling everyone what they are supposed to do." My toes curled upon hearing these words, but I managed to ask the elder what he meant. He replied, "That is what the pastor is supposed to do." I pointed out that although this was how pastors in this congregation's history had traditionally led, it was not my leadership style. Our conversation revealed that the collaborative, holistic, relationship-centered style of leadership that is ingrained in

who I am (not just because I am a woman) was new to their
understanding of pastoral leadership.

Initially, I desperately wanted to avoid having conversations
about my identity and how it influenced the ways I exhibited
pastoral leadership as a "woman pastor," because I was afraid
people would pigeonhole me and find reinforcement for their
assumptions that I wouldn't be able to do a "man's job." I eventually discovered that these conversations had been important
in my helping to overcome ingrained assumptions on the part
of the congregation about what the responsibilities and leadership style of pastor (male or female) are in a particular context.
As *the* woman pastor in a congregation, I talked regularly with
the congregation about how gender stereotypes influence the
assumptions of what a pastor will be and do.

The conversations between the congregation and me have
also touched on the blessing and challenge that in calling a
woman pastor, the members of the congregation told one another that they were they were ready for a change. They sensed
that God was calling them to do and be something outside
their comfort zone, and they acted on that conviction by calling a female clergyperson. They had no idea how that would
affect their congregational identity and ministry. The step itself
was an indicator of openness to God's vision for the church of
which they may not have been fully aware.

One of the effects my presence had on the congregation in
this small town was that it gained a reputation as the "liberal"
church because it had a woman in the pulpit. Congregation
members joked that at a dinner party or in line at the grocery
store acquaintances would comment that "it must be interesting to hear sermons from a woman." Some people would even
go so far as to ask, "When are you going to get a *real* pastor?—
because my church says that women aren't allowed to lead
churches."

In part, I knew that these kinds of conversations were going
on because of the attitudes I saw displayed toward me by other

local clergy. When I first came to this rural small town and tried to attend the monthly meetings of the town's ministerial association, it took two months for me to find out where the group was meeting. Every time I called one of the pastors, he would give me the runaround about not being sure where they were meeting that particular month. I was excited for the opportunity to build collegial relationships with other clergy in town, though I don't believe the prospect of a "lady minister" invading their boys' club appealed to them in the same way it did to me. When I tracked them down and showed up, the men shifted uncomfortably in their chairs as I joined them. Never did they ask me to pray. Never was I asked for my opinion concerning theological or social concerns facing our larger community.

No matter how much I wanted to avoid having conversations about my identity as a "woman pastor"—because I was afraid that talking about it would only reinforce people's assumptions that I wouldn't be able to do a "man's job"—the conversation was unavoidable. It didn't matter that I wasn't talking about it; someone else was. By being open and honest with the congregation about my experiences and how the parishioners felt about the community's perception of them as a church, our communication with one another helped them to be transformed into the community God was calling them to be. And those conversations helped me to reflect on my pastoral identity.

Reaching Out to My Sisters

As beneficial as those conversations were for my ministry with the congregation, I quickly came to realize that they weren't enough to be a sustainable support for my growth as a pastor. Systems of support (however they look) are crucial when you are *the* pastor. I didn't have the convenience of having another pastor on staff with whom to engage in conversation about troublesome situations, theological conundrums, or the random rants of everyday life as a minister. Building systems of support takes intentional, and more often than not, creative effort. These systems of support can take many forms. When I first started serving in my new call, I thought it couldn't be *that* hard to find others pastors who were flying solo, serving as *the* woman pastor, and located in churches less than a day's drive from me. That perception couldn't have been further from reality. When I started serving my first congregation, I was stunned to learn I was the only female Presbyterian pastor under the age of fifty in my presbytery. Although I am thankful for the mentoring and support I received from the experienced women in the area, I learned never to underestimate the power of technology to create systems of support. Through websites such as Facebook and Twitter, I was able to find other young women who were serving in their first calls as solo pastors. These relationships have been the most significant for me in my own journey as a new pastor. We formed bonds, 140 characters at a time, around our passion for preaching, struggles with presiding over our first funeral, and frustration that no one ever read the church newsletter we spent hours putting together.

Many of the friends and colleagues with whom I graduated from seminary have already left ministry or are seriously contemplating seeking a new vocation. It is not hard for me to identify with some of their frustrations, including those I have given voice to in this chapter: experiencing loneliness, struggling with pastoral identity, having your authority challenged because you are a woman, and coming to terms with some of the "grunt work" that is part of everyday ministry. In the midst of those challenges, I have been sustained by connections to friends and colleagues who are willing to be honest about the challenges they face as solo pastors and as women. But on an even more profound level, I have celebrated that God kept showing up. God kept showing up at the pulpit, font, and table.

God kept showing up at my doorstep. God kept showing up around tables, hospital beds, and graves. God kept showing up for another cup of coffee.

The Girlfriends' Checklist

- As you begin your search, pay attention to the areas of ministry that you feel called to or want more experience doing.
- Put into place systems of accountability for your job performance. Be sure you and the personnel committee or governing board have an up-to-date job description and conduct annual reviews.
- Identify ways you can create spiritual, personal, and emotional support for your ministry with individuals or groups *outside* the church.

·3·

The Eternal Associate

WORKING FOR THE WOMAN UPSTAIRS, NOT THE MAN DOWN THE HALL

*Marianne J. Grano, Amy Morgan,
and Amanda Adams Riley*

• • • •

As you and God seek your "match made in heaven," as Amy so nicely put it, you are probably looking at a call as a solo pastor or associate. Although a young woman was suitable to bear the Son of God, generally young people are not viewed as possessing the necessary experience needed for the big head-pastor position. And given the learning curve of our own first few years in ordained ministry, we can say that experience can make a huge difference. Most young women coming out of seminary will find themselves seeking their first call as a solo pastor of a small church, as an associate pastor in a larger church, or working in a specialized ministry (such as chaplaincy).

In discerning what type of first call you will seek, you will need to consider your personality, your gifts for ministry, and your goals in ministry, because—although you may fear otherwise, and some may disagree—the associate need not be your eternal role! Some of us feel called to associate ministry (chaplaincy, or work on any kind of staff) because we enjoy the collaboration with other pastoral staff. Associate ministry also allows us to focus our ministry work in a specific area. Finally, being an associate gives us the time to grow in experience as well as to share the burdens of ministry. For an associate, there are benefits and challenges to our unique calling.

Enjoying Big-Church Culture

Small churches are wonderful places in which rich ministries flourish, and Melissa described very well all of the pluses in the solo pastor's life in such settings. Yet the small church is just not the context in which some of us fit. We like to look out at a lot of people in the sanctuary. We like to know that there are established programs for children and youth. We like the programs and ministries that are possible in a church with several hundred members. If you believe your calling is to be a head pastor, traditional models of ministry teach that an associate position is a good place in which to learn the workings of the larger church. If you grew up in a corporate-size church (401–1000 members), you may feel most comfortable in a church of a similar size. Likewise, if you grew up in a program-size congregation (251–400 members), that may be where you see yourself functioning most easily. The size and the organizational structure of a church have an important bearing on the way ministry will operate there. You will learn a great deal about how large churches run day to day by working in one. And, as a graduate fresh out of seminary, if you work in one, it will likely be as an associate.

Receiving the Guidance of a Head Pastor

When you consider potential calls, make sure that you pay close attention to the head pastor of the church. He (and it will probably be a *he*) will most likely invite you to lunch or to a special interview. If he does not, make sure you get one-on-one time with him before accepting the position. Consider his personality, theology, and questions for and about you. Try to get a sense of his leadership and management style. Is he a micromanager, and if so, can you live with that? Is he "type A," and can you work well with someone who is or isn't? How flexible is he, and how flexible are you? When does he take his day off, and how does he balance ministry and personal time? This conversation will teach you about his expectations of himself as they relate to work, and potentially his expectations of you. Ask him how he has handled difficult staff situations, because there always will be challenges, and you want to know that he will not play favorites or throw you under the bus when things get bad. Imagine his reactions to various situations in your ministry and life. For example, if the due date of your first child turned out to be December 25, would this person completely freak out?

If you meet a head pastor whose theology and personality mesh with your own, who would not freak out—at least not in front of you—when you encounter challenges in ministry (which you will), who will support you publicly in the church, and from whom you think you could gain wisdom, you should consider the call, even if there are other reasons for hesitation. When you are having conversations with him, listen to the way he talks about other staff and previous staff. This is likely how he will talk about you if you serve there. Then, ask around the regional governing body about the head of staff's reputation. (You can learn a lot from doing your homework.) As an associate, your relationship with the head pastor will be one of the most important factors, perhaps the most important factor, determining whether you will be happy and fruitful in ministry. The head pastor will be your supervisor and will conduct your annual review. If you have major hesitations about this person, you should consider not taking a call for this reason. We have all turned down calls because of reservations about the head of staff, and we have friends who haven't. It can be a bad scene if you find yourself in a situation with a challenging head of staff.

Marianne has the blessing of working with a head pastor whose personality and theology mesh with her own, whom she considers to be wise and to have a lot of insight about ministry, and who has been very supportive, even when she told him her baby's due date was January 13—and he had been planning to take the whole month of January as vacation. Once a church member was talking with Marianne and the head of staff and joked that it would really help the organ fund if Marianne were to take a year without salary. The pastor responded, "Did you know that Marianne is one of the lowest-paid ministers in our presbytery? Do you think that is commensurate with her level of skill and the hours that she works?" Having this kind of support in ministry is really important, and you should be thankful to be an associate working with such a person.

Amy is also in a healthy associate pastor relationship with her head of staff. She also knows what can happen when the associate pastor does not have a wise and supportive head of staff to work with, however. Amy came into her first call three weeks after the head of staff left. Her first two years of ministry were lived out in an interim period when there was sometimes another gifted, compassionate, and experienced associate, sometimes a less-than-perfect interim head of staff, and sometimes neither. Surviving her first years in ministry without strong leadership and guidance was an overwhelming challenge at times. But those difficult years also revealed an additional benefit of serving as an associate in a large-membership church: you have other staff members to rely on, even if there isn't a head of staff in place with whom you jell completely. The supportive and gifted staff at Amy's church helped her survive and thrive through her first two years and prepared her to be a better associate pastor when the new head of staff arrived.

Amanda has had the blessing of serving under two head pastors in two congregations. She learned lots from both men, and while neither has the same personality type as she does, both modeled and taught her what good ministry consists of when you are not the overly eager "type A" personality. Serving with these two clergy allowed her to deepen her pastoral knowledge and to practice being a calm presence in the midst of adverse situations, as well as learning what it takes to stay in ministry long term.

Specializing in an Area of Ministry

Associate pastors tend to be associates in something, whether it is youth ministry, pastoral care, adult education, children's ministries, or any other area a church can dream up. A person who is really a pastoral type might be best suited for an associate position in pastoral care. Another person who is gifted in education might flourish in an associate position in Christian education. Many of the positions you will find include youth ministry, the most common role an associate fills. Amanda, Amy, and Marianne have all been responsible for youth programs or are currently serving as "youth pastor," and there are great joys in getting to know the youth in a special and personal way. As a youth, Marianne liked going on mission trips and confirmation retreats. Now she gets paid to do it.

Some associate pastor positions are more generalized, especially in program-size churches. You might get the opportunity to preach regularly; assist in pastoral care, weddings, and funerals; lead committees; and administer programs. This is all good training for those who might hope eventually to move into a head-of-staff position, or even to a solo or a more specialized associate position. Be aware, however, that these positions can be the dumping ground for whatever pastoral or administrative tasks the head of staff is less than fond of. If you think you might someday be called to be a senior or solo pastor, it may be wise to be intentional about preaching regularly, so that your skills stay sharp. Common wisdom says that preaching monthly will keep your preaching muscles toned while serving as an associate. When interviewing for an associate pastor position, particularly a generalized one, make sure your job description is clear about your roles and responsibilities. Being an associate pastor is an important and unique calling. It is not merely a training ground for head pastors. Nor is an associate a personal assistant for the head of staff. If you find yourself researching all-inclusive resorts for your head of staff's family vacation, you might have missed your calling.

Having an Instant Set of Office Friends

One thing you will like about being an associate in a multistaff church is that you have an instant set of, if not "friend-friends," at least coworker friends. You can drop by the church office and talk to the secretarial staff members about Thanksgiving plans. You can laugh it up at staff meetings. People called to work in the same church as you will share your faith and many of your views on life. As Amy mentioned, we have found that these people can be wonderful sources of support and fellowship.

Now, a church staff is like a family in that you could end up in a functional one or a dysfunctional one. You may end up on a staff that is so riddled with personality conflicts that you need another set of friends with whom it is safe to talk about the church. But come to think of it, that's a good set of friends to have in any case!

Relating to the Head of Staff

As the subtitle of this chapter suggests, as an associate you will find fulfillment in ministry if you remember that you work for God (the Woman upstairs), not the senior pastor (the man down the hall). At the same time, we must again stress that as an associate, your relationship with the head of staff will be important to your joy in ministry. The head pastor may direct when you will take your vacation or how you will respond to the disgruntled mom of one of the youth. In most churches he will be your supervisor, and you will need to check in with him regularly, if only to go over who will do what in the service on Sunday. The way this working relationship develops will depend on his personality and yours, whether you communicate frequently through e-mail or other channels, and whether you have a regular check-in time or just drop in to one another's offices when it is convenient.

The degree to which the head pastor functions as a boss or as a partner will be a function mostly of his style and of the culture of the church. This is something you will want to figure out before you take the call. While associates typically preach when the head pastor wants them to preach and take vacation when the head pastor wants them to take vacation, you may find that your head of staff is more flexible and willing to work with you. The church staffs on which the three of us work are much more on the collegial side. We feel comfortable even disagreeing with the head of staff as to whether an idea will work. You may have a more formal working relationship, or you may be on friendly terms with the head of staff, even able to ask for direction in your personal life.

Female associates in particular need to deal with specific issues that will arise if your head of staff is male, which is likely the case. During one short period, one of us was supervised by another woman, but we recognize that this is rare. Indeed, all three of us are now serving in two-pastor churches with an older male head of staff. We have heard horror stories about this situation, which is quite common. One young clergywoman reported that her head of staff jokingly referred to her, in public, as his "second wife." Another head pastor once referred to his wife and the associate as "the two women in my life."

These types of inappropriate comments demonstrate the importance of reinforcing boundaries in your relationship with the head of staff. As a young woman, you are already viewed by society as a sexual and reproductive commodity. No one should have the opportunity to picture an inappropriate relationship between you and anyone else in the church, especially the head pastor. Make sure that the door is left open when you are conversing alone with the head of staff, or be sure to have conversations in rooms with windows in the doors. Consider carefully whether you will make it a practice to go out for lunch, coffee, or dinner with him. Some of us feel comfortable with a working lunch, while others do not.

Also—and this is something you may not hear about in seminary—you will need to establish a friendly relationship with the pastor's wife, if he is married. We have seen this relationship go in many different directions, from friendship to toleration to hostility, and have even heard of pastors' wives who oppose women's ordination to ministry. Marianne is in the interesting position of having the pastor's wife as a colleague on staff. Especially if the pastor has never had a female associate before, the pastor's wife may feel threatened by your position in the life of her husband or in the life of the church. From the beginning, show her that you value her position, her guidance, and her support of you in life and ministry. It is always better to have her on your side than against you, and she can be your ally as you work with her husband and grow to better understand him.

Basically your relationship with the head of staff and his family is an extension of everything we hope you have learned up to this point in your life about interpersonal relations, but more so. Why more so? In a church, there is a blurring of the personal and professional that is not common in many other professions. Again, a church is like a family, and we have observed that a multistaff church could allow the surfacing of what you (and all the other members of staff) learned in your own family of origin.

Relating to Other Staff Members

If you are an associate pastor, you may be working in a multi-staff church that has several other pastoral or lay program staff members as well as support staff. The way these people work with one another is a function of their own personalities. The congregation also has its own institutional memory or spiritual background. Some churches have a history of disagreement among the staff—of associate pastors always leaving after three years, or the music director's not getting along with the mission coordinator, or the sexton's being disagreeable to everyone. In Amy's church, there was an unhealthy history of an "us-versus-them" mentality between the staff and the congregational leaders. Furthermore, over the past couple of decades, heads of staff had experienced brief tenures, while associates seemed to stay forever. While these patterns can be changed, you first need to know what the patterns are. Find out about the history of the church staff, so that you know what you are walking into. If you are not the first associate at the church, it is worth having a conversation with the person who filled the role before you, even if it was ten years ago.

When it comes to relationships with other staff members, there is great value in simple principles. For example, listen to the points of view of other staff members. When you are a younger person, some staff will assume that you are a totally naive, starry-eyed seminary dreamer. To some extent, they are correct. Let them know that their experience in working in the church is valuable. You may want to change things right away, but there may be valid reasons why "we've always done it this way." There is still a certain power in the title of pastor, as often reflected in salary and benefits packages, but program staff who are not ordained, you will find, are still ministers who have incredible gifts to offer the church. Learn from them and from the other associates. Foster relationships with members of the staff outside of church; go out together to events that involve church members; remember staff birthdays. You are in a position as a young woman to bring a lot of energy, enthusiasm, and new ideas for serving God into the church staff, as well as into the church itself. You will be able to do this much more effectively if you see yourself working as part of a team rather than on your own. This team atmosphere is one of the greatest benefits (or challenges, depending on your perspective and the team you're working with) of serving as an associate pastor.

Your Role in the Church

It's helpful to remember that the church as a whole works as a team, too. If you are an associate, you already know that you are not in charge of the church—don't you? If not, you are in for a rude awakening. You probably have ideas about the way things could be done, fresh-out-of-seminary ideals about new ways of being church. So you go to your first mission committee meeting and begin to talk about your ideas for an international social-justice and peacemaking project. You then learn that most of the people on the committee don't believe you should engage in any work outside a ten-mile radius of the church, because "giving begins at home." You will have more success if you first take time to find out where the church's mindset is, and meet the people at that point. Remember that the pastor is a shepherd, and you can't shepherd people if you are running out ahead of them. Learn to walk beside the church. Recognize that in many churches, you are approximately the age of most church members' grandkids. The granddaughter is generally not the person who challenges people—but she can be, if she does so in the right way. Many people are much more willing to listen to their grandchildren than they are to their children. You may not be granted the automatic power of an older, male head of staff. You will be heard better if you offer your thoughts and ideas in the context of a relationship in which you also show support for other people's ideas, not just in words but in actions. Lift up others' ideas in worship, the area over which pastors possibly have the most control.

While the bad part is that the granddaughter is not automatically thought of as the person in charge, the good part is that the granddaughter is automatically the recipient of love. You are a sign of new life to many younger and older people in the church. There will be people in the church, even people who are not related to your area of ministry at all, who will just love you. This is one of the places in ministry from which you will derive a great deal of joy, as you feel surrounded by their love and support. Moments when we have felt overwhelmed by this love are when experiencing transitions in life—receiving hundreds of wedding gifts, baby gifts, and sympathy cards. Another is the thank-you notes we receive from people whose lives we have touched. Keep the thank-you notes in a file or on a shelf. Read them when you are feeling down. You are making a difference in people's lives. You are bringing people closer to God. There is a reason why *you* are doing *this*.

Notes for Young Women Youth Pastors

Here are a few notes for the particular situation of young women in youth ministry. Youth ministry may end up being your calling for a time, even if you do not feel that it is your gift. This is because you happen to be young and churches happen to want young pastors who can work with youth. As a young woman, you face particular challenges in youth ministry. You might be smaller than some of the twelfth-grade boys or even the eleventh-grade girls, which can present a problem in the area of discipline. You might not command the instant attention and respect of a 32-year-old "cool" male youth leader. These challenges open the way for you to have a youth ministry that is not about you but about God. You do not need to have a personality cult; you need to help build these young people into followers of Christ. Part of this task is creating a safe space where youth experience consistency and caring, where they can feel a sense of trust in one another and in the adults—plural—serving them.

The most important thing we each believe we have done so far in youth ministry is to recruit the right people as youth leaders. You are not the center of the youth ministry. God is the center, and there needs to be a team of people of both genders and at least three generations leading people toward that center. Identify men—and women, but especially men—in the church who have some strengths that you do not. When Marianne took high-school students to Jamaica on a mission trip, the people at Immigration did not believe she was the pastor of the church. She was thankful to have a sixty-something youth leader to pose as group leader on the return trip. Identify an adult coleader for the youth group who can be the "cool" guy who tells jokes and makes things fun in the youth group, one who can represent a voice of experience kids will listen to (a lot of youth will respect people their grandparents' age and think they are cool), one who knows how to build things or who is a good driver, or who can discipline, or who can lead Bible studies.

It is important that you learn ways to be in ministry both with young women who will look to you as an example and with young men with whom you will have to find a way to relate, whether it is through a shared football team or television show, or as a respected older sister or aunt. Again, boundaries are important. A youth might have a crush on you, and you need to behave appropriately at all times. You are a young person, but you are not these young people's friend: you are their spiritual leader. When you get the hard questions and the tough phone calls, you will be glad that they see you as a person able to help them in their relationship with God.

Eternal God . . . Temporary Calling

Most women in ordained ministry tend to be associates. It is no secret that there is a "stained-glass ceiling." In those denominations that are ordaining women, there are still few women in positions as heads of staff, especially in the largest tall-steeple churches. There are several reasons for this state of affairs. One is that women are still the minority among clergy, and large numbers have not been ordained long enough to rise to the positions of heads of staff. Another reason is that since the ordination of women, many women ministers have left full-time ministry because of the difficulty of balancing work and family life, because their spouses are tied to a job in a specific geographic area and they cannot move as freely as some men, or because of other reasons, including burnout.

We must also be honest that there still exists in the church a level of comfort in having a man as the head of staff. Church search committees seeking a new head pastor have an image in their heads, even if only on a subconscious level. There is subtle discrimination, not only against women but also against ministers of color, ministers with disabilities, and even ministers who are short. There are similar reasons why many women do not become solo pastors—the inability of a spouse to relocate, a tendency to work collegially and a reluctance to work independently, or feelings of inadequacy at being *the* pastor. Many young women ordained into ministry today seek to "shatter the stained-glass ceiling" by gaining the skills and experience necessary as an associate to be called into these positions of greater influence within the church. Many men entering ministry also see the associate position as a stepping-stone to another call. I have heard older men say frankly, "I only stayed in that position a few years because I was an associate. I wanted my own church."

While we must be conscious that no church is *ever* "our own church," thank God, it is also healthy to recognize that all callings in ministry are only temporary. Even our last call is only a stop along the journey, not our final destination. We emphasize this because many of us, looking out at the prevailing position of women in ministry, believe we are destined to be the eternal associate and cannot even imagine an alternative. There are many alternatives to the associate position outside congregation-based ministry: ministries in the denomination, mission, chaplaincy, communication, education in colleges and seminaries, and many more. In the church, you may be called at a different time to solo, head pastor, or copastor positions.

Whatever vision you have in mind, or even if you are blessed to feel that the associate call you have found is a perfect match for the foreseeable future, it is a good idea to be open to God's direction. Several people in Marianne's life—all men, actually—keep suggesting head pastor positions in churches that they just *know* she is called to. It doesn't seem to matter to them that she is pretty happy serving God where she is, that she knows that her ministry becomes more effective the longer she stays in this church, and that she can really imagine only a few months into the future and leaves the rest to God. Leaving the rest to God, however, means allowing yourself to be open to hearing God's voice wherever God calls, even if that call is uncomfortable and a little scary. After years of feeling called to solo or head of staff ministry, Amanda has settled into understanding that God's call comes in many different forms, and has come to appreciate and love her role as an associate. While she believes she is not an "eternal" associate, she also knows that her gifts for ministry and her call can be employed in a multitude of settings.

Finally, we want to emphasize that the position of associate pastor can be a unique and wonderful calling. While many pastors, like their secular counterparts, feel the need to "work their way up," not all of us do. Amy's goals for life and ministry don't include serving as senior pastor of the large-membership church where she currently ministers. She's actually quite happy to let her head of staff do that. She is blessed to be able to serve in the areas of ministry she is most gifted in, not having to be all things to all people, and learning to establish healthy boundaries in her family and personal life while serving in ministry. For Amy, being the eternal associate sounds like a lovely prospect.

Some churches are blessed by associates who serve very long tenures, lasting through numerous changes in top leadership. Like any long-term calling, this one allows the associate to grow in her gifts and skills, in her relationship with the church and its members, and in her ministry role. Depending on your gifts, personality, and life goals, these things can far outweigh the status and larger paycheck that come with "moving up the ladder." No matter what form your ministry takes, as an associate or otherwise, remember that just as God's work in this world is not done, neither is God's call and claim on your life. In a forty-year career, your call will change and grow as you respond to God's continued work in this world.

The Girlfriends' Checklist

- Consider an associate call for larger churches, specialized ministries, mentorship, and friends.
- If you get a great vibe from the head pastor, consider taking the call. If you get a bad vibe from the head pastor, consider *not* taking the call.
- Be extraordinarily careful with boundaries with the head of staff and others in the church.
- Remember that the church staff is a family, whether functional or dysfunctional.
- If you are in youth ministry, recruit a diverse team. Find males who can be what you are not, find a way to relate to young men—and keep the boundaries in place!
- Keep in mind that you do not need to be the eternal associate! Be open to God's call in your life and to a variety of possible ministries in your future.

·4·

Pastors on Parade

OWNING YOUR EMBODIED MINISTRY

Marianne J. Grano

• • • •

One thing you will come to appreciate in ministry is the special parking spaces some hospitals reserve for pastors. Some hospitals also have Stork Parking for pregnant women, so when I was pregnant, I wondered if pregnant pastors got some kind of double extra-special space. Or maybe they just let you drive right into the front lobby.

One day on a hospital visit, I parked in the pastor's spot as I normally did and began to walk into the hospital. As I was doing so, a man stopped me and said, "You know, that parking spot is for pastors." I couldn't think of a good comeback. Perhaps, "Where do the sexist pigs park? Maybe they have a spot for you." Hindsight is 20/20. All I said was, "Yes, I know." And I walked on.

How many times can you hear "You look so young!" and not bite off the head of the person who said it? I would like to pull out my credentials, my diplomas, my Greek and Hebrew exams, my SAT scores every time someone says that. And it happens every day. And no matter what, I believe that when people say, "You look so young!" they are also saying, "You look so female!" The fact is that I am not what people expect to see in the pulpit or the pastor's parking spot. The fact is that most people did not grow up with a woman in the pulpit, and particularly not a twenty-four-year-old woman—my age when I was ordained.

During my clinical pastoral education (CPE), I came to terms with the fact that I would constantly have to deal with people's surprise at my appearance. Young women are traditionally expected to get married and have babies. I did my CPE in the mother-baby unit of a large hospital. Of course, it makes sense that a woman would be sent to that unit, as women were often breastfeeding or in various stages of undress, and a man might feel uncomfortable or cause a woman to feel uncomfortable. But many times as I was visiting women and their babies, I was asked whether I had children or would be having children. I know a man could have been asked the same question, but somehow I wonder if he would be asked so often. I also heard, constantly, "You look so young!" And I *was* young. I am still young, at twenty-nine.

I am young, but so was Jesus, thirty-three at his crucifixion. So was David, thirty when he became king. Martin Luther King, Jr., was thirty-five when he received the Nobel Prize. And Mary was only a teenager when she gave birth to the Son of God.

Walking with Mary

Perhaps it was a result of being around all that childbirth; in any case, during my summer in the mother-baby unit, I began an intense spiritual relationship with Mary—a bit strange, perhaps, for a Protestant. Yet it was not so much her holiness that captivated me as the way she had been chosen as a young woman for a great task. Kenda Creasy Dean and Ron Foster contrast Mary, a teenage girl, with Zechariah, an older man, in their wonderful book on youth ministry, *The Godbearing Life*: "Zechariah, defined by his adult commitments, had difficulty receiving God's surprising grace. . . . But Mary, a poor, unmarried teenage girl, has no preconceived identity apart from that endowed by her creator. While Zechariah's reluctance to believe led to silence, Mary's malleability before God erupts in song."[1] Dean and Foster point out that the young, like Mary, possess an openness to God's working in the world in new and different ways.

Our culture idolizes youthful appearances, but, particularly in the church, there is also a bias toward people with "more experience" and not much value placed on the fresh perspective a young person can bring. I have actually read listings of churches seeking a pastor describing the ideal candidate as "young at heart." Such a description precludes the possibility that the pastor will actually *be* young. As many of our churches are themselves aging, they find it difficult to consider a young person as someone who can walk beside them, let alone lead them. Indeed, I have heard young women colleagues whose congregations complain that a thirty-year-old woman cannot understand what the congregation is experiencing. Yet how does the church expect to engage young people without being open to their input and leadership? Is it possible that a pastor who might look and sound a little different might, like Mary, be the bearer of new life?

As I continued my spiritual walk with Mary, I found myself increasingly comfortable in my own skin, as a young woman whom God could use to do new things. I began to see the image of weakness that my young, small, female body conveyed to actually be my strength. I realized that few people were intimidated by the image I presented—a situation that made it possible for people to open up to me. This was the case not only with young women, but even with older males, who wept in my presence that summer and who opened their hearts and feelings to me in a way that I believe would have been more dif-

ficult if I had exuded an aura of power. Like Mary, my power-
lessness in the eyes of the world made me the handmaid of the
Lord, ready to serve in whatever way God directed me.

Having Style

I had never thought much about my hair until I went to seminary. When I started seminary and began envisioning myself
as a clergyperson, I started looking at the style of women pastors, particularly women head pastors, as I have always had an
ambitious streak. And I noticed that virtually without excep-
tion, they had "The Haircut." The Don't-Think-of-Me-as-a-
Woman-Think-of-Me-as-a-Pastor haircut—short, shapeless,
unfeminine. In most cases, I imagine that being a head pastor
would take up so much time and create so much stress that hair
(along with fashion in general) really did not make the list of
daily priorities. Yet at the same time, as my classmates began to
take on internships, and as I noticed more and more of them
getting the snip, my hair began to take on Samson-like power
in my mind, and I feared the day when I would have to lose it.
Could I be a pastor, and still be feminine, long-haired *me*?

I am, gender-wise, extraordinarily feminine. I was a cheerleader in high school. In my senior year, I was actually the only
cheerleader in the school's calculus class. I stood out on game
days in my miniskirt and curly beribboned ponytail, doing
integrations at my desk. I moved between two worlds. And I
learned just as much from cheerleading—through the sweaty,
painful practices leading to glorious stunts and dance and gym-
nastics, all with smiles on mouths lipsticked with the team's
uniform shade—as I did in calculus. I was used to people assuming that I was an idiot in calculus and assuming that I was
a nerd in cheerleading.

I found that seminary is definitely more of a calculus kind
of place. There was a sort of uniform of jeans and earth-toned
sweaters. There were no miniskirts, and definitely no ribbons.
Even in our schoolwork, there was some kind of honor, I of-

ten felt, in being as humdrum as possible. While most of my classmates would simply read their papers aloud and call it a "presentation," my presentations had visuals, interactive components, sometimes food, and I was even known to incorporate clips from popular television shows such as *Friends*. I attained a reputation for what one of my fellow students called "style over substance."

So I rebelled by being myself—a girl. Without really thinking about it, I started wearing more skirts to class. And more pink. And more heels. And my hair just grew and grew. By the time I graduated, it reached to my waist—long, straight, and blonde, blonde, blonde.

Reality set in when I began the call process. Faced with the prospect of life without health insurance, I nearly lost my faith—in long hair, I mean. After much trial and error, I pretty much perfected the bun, figuring I could keep my hair a non-issue in front of the church and let my girly self shine in the rest of my life. I tried to hide my pink purse and heart keychain as quickly as possible during the interviews.

Eventually God called me to a wonderful church, a church where I really felt I could be myself. Still, I kept the bun on Sundays, waging war against gravity with dozens of bobby pins and gallons of hairspray, and I put my hair up in some way every other day of the week. Yet every once in a while a congregation member would literally catch me with my hair down, and never did that individual fail to comment on its length and beauty— perhaps less because my hair was actually beautiful than because it was such a shock to see this evidence of my other self. I managed to live this kind of divided life—although I got a more conservative black purse—all the way until I traveled to Ireland with the youth choir. The demands of daily travel and jet lag won over the bun. At the ongoing requests of churchgoers to see the hair, I relented and let it flow. But when Sunday came around again, I felt a terrible compulsion to put it back up. I felt that I had to look professional—meaning conservative and not too feminine—for the sake of the congregation.

When I went out to lunch one day after church, I pondered this with three people I love. Two of these people were women judges in their fifties, products of feminism's second wave, when upper-middle-class white women began to seek careers outside the home. They were among the few women in their courses at law school, and they related stories about being mistaken for secretaries at law firm meetings. To be valued in the workplace, they were often forced to fit the masculine definition of how a professional spoke, acted, and dressed. The third person with me was my husband. When the conversation turned to my hair, interestingly, the judges were adamant that I should keep the bun. It is more professional, they said. Just as adamantly, my husband advocated for the letting down of my hair. His attitude was that I should be the "real me" with the congregation. I should be me, and I should show my style.

All this led me to think, more and more, about questions of style and substance. I believe that in many historic Protestant churches, we are afraid of style. In our hearts of hearts, many of us believe that style is for the megachurches. Style is for the black church. Style is for the Catholics. At best, this tradition of dullness speaks out against the idolatry of style. After all, style is the god of our culture, which I would argue worships the image more than any other culture ever has. Between TV, the Internet, and digital billboards, we are flooded each day with flashy eye-candy that does not invite deep reflection—no wonder so many churches resist putting up a projection screen at the front of the sanctuary, fearing their worship will become "commercials for Jesus."

Yet this attitude of substance-over-style can become elitist. It is yet another incarnation of what Rosemary Radford Ruether described in *Sexism and God-Talk* as the dichotomization of material and spiritual energy.[2] Ruether recognizes that all women, including women of the dominant race and class, have often been identified with the "matter" side of the equation. So have female and male people of color, the poor, and nature itself. And I believe this identification of women as "matter," as

"style," continues in the way that women are viewed professionally, particularly in ministry. The more people consider our appearance, the less they consider what we are actually saying. We
are subject to scrutiny for our style. Sometimes when I'm up
in front of the church with the older male head of staff, I feel
like Kelly on the show *Live with Regis and Kelly*. Nobody really
notices what Regis is wearing, but we all evaluate what Kelly is
sporting. People comment on my shoes, my jewelry, my hair, of
course, and what I might be wearing under my robe. I am un-
abashedly viewed as matter, as style. And I know from my conversations with other young clergywomen that this experience
is a universal one for our set. Male pastors and older women are
definitely subject to scrutiny for what they wear. Yet younger
women are particularly subject to being viewed for their style
because television and the media promote young women as ob-
jects. Thus I have sometimes felt that my style is more important to the congregation than what I am saying about God. I
wonder if I should keep my "girliness" out of the pulpit, so that
people will direct their attention to spiritual matters. I wonder
if I should keep the hair up.

"Style" speaks to the senses. "Substance" speaks to the
mind. We have been taught to divorce the two, never trying
to manipulate our audience by invoking the material. Yet my
style-over-substance critics never recognized that even their
black-and-white, two-dimensional presentations inhabited
the world of matter. Their ascetic simplicity spoke volumes in
itself—but they never recognized this reality. I have seen the
same thing, all too often, in the pulpit—sermons meant to con-
vince listeners intellectually of a particular theological point,
but that made little reference to the sights, sounds, and experiences of the listeners' actual lives. While in seminary, I took a
course called "Preaching as Celebration," which taught preaching from the black church tradition, instead of the regular
(white) preaching course, mostly because I was sick of boring
sermons and wanted an alternative. There, Frank A. Thomas
taught, "Western homiletical thought, based on cerebral pro-

cess, has been overly concerned with content."[3] Thomas taught that Jesus had content, but Jesus had sense appeal, too. Jesus talked about real-life experiences, wineskins, and wells. Thomas taught me, from his own tradition of the black church, about the holiness of the interaction of substance and style.

I believe we as young women have an opportunity to own this holy interaction, this incarnation, as part of our ministries. From my many conversations with young women clergy on this subject, I have concluded that as a young woman, you will never get away from being looked at. But you have some control over what people will see. We have an opportunity to have a ministry of style. We have an opportunity to show our style, to own our style, to be intentional with our style, and to allow our style to redefine what it means to be a child of God, a Christian, or a minister of Word and Sacrament. God called you, so be yourself. For some of you, being yourself means going without makeup, even without shaving, and telling your congregants, well, this is how God made me. For others it will mean becoming a welcoming congregation to some nontraditional members with dyed hair and nose rings. For me, it is proclaiming, in my pink, my high heels, and my cute skirts that yes, I am a minister, and yes, I am a girl.

Your Pastoral Authority

My first sermon was titled "Salvation for Short People" and was on the story of Zacchaeus, who was so short that he had to climb a tree to see Jesus. It was preached in a historic church with an ornate Gothic sanctuary. I came to the preacher's chair and sat down; at five foot three, I found that my feet dangled, inches from the floor. I felt a great kinship to Zacchaeus that day.

Then at my current congregation, when our sanctuary was going to be renovated, the renovation committee decided on a transparent pulpit. I asked about the height issue with such a pulpit. How high was the pulpit going to be, I asked, and how would it be adjusted for shorter people? It was suggested that a box be placed under the pulpit for me to stand on—pretty embarrassing with a transparent pulpit! It may as well have been a telephone book! I heard the story of another congregation that built its new pulpit to fit the male senior pastor, who was over six feet tall. He subsequently left as soon as the renovation was complete, leaving behind two female associates, neither of whom fit the pulpit. The "desk" part of the pulpit should be adjustable to various heights whenever a congregation installs a new pulpit. Congregations ought to consider the participation of women, youth, children, and people with disabilities when they make these decisions.

If you are a shorter person, as many of us women are, you may find you feel "shortchanged" in the ministry. This can be another source of stress for a woman or anyone who is short. Many people, even subconsciously, equate height with power. I have even noticed that some "tall-steeple" churches tend to hire "tall-steeple" pastors.

If you are seeking to add some authority to your embodied ministry, you are probably excited about the prospect of buying robes, or albs, or cassocks and surplices, or other liturgical vestments, and clergy shirts. You may envision that they will give you that look of spiritual clout. Even though you may not look as people expect you to look when they think "pastor," the collar will set them straight. The robe will convey your ministerial dignity.

I believe that the "robe" of ministry is more than just a garment. Since being ordained, I have kept my style, it's true. I am still me, and I am still a girl. But I have a new role. This role has changed every relationship in my life. It changes how people react to me at parties, and it changes how I act at those parties. It changed my name—I now have the title "Rev." As George Herbert's poem "The Collar" suggests, the ministry changes who you are and who you can be. He laments, "Shall I still be in

suit?" and rails, "Forsake thy cage, Thy rope of sands."⁴ The key
is to find the "robe" that works for you.

If you choose to wear a robe or other clergy vestments, I
recommend purchasing ones that are cut to fit you, and not
a broad-shouldered man, and that you find attractive. It is
important that your robe fit who you are. God called you to
the ministry, and so you are still you, just in a new role and a
new robe. Also, young ladies, on a practical note, think about
whether this robe may need to fit through a pregnancy!

Also, while I absolutely believe in keeping a personal style,
and in owning my embodied ministry, and being myself, I have
noticed that the ministry has changed me, and has changed
my style. When I was ordained, I had my favorite pair of pink
pants that I wore all the time. They were very girly, and very me.
One day I received a call at my desk. It was from a parishioner
whose brother had just committed suicide. I said I would be
right over, and then I realized I was wearing the pink pants. I
did not feel comfortable wearing those pants on that occasion,
so, being far from my home, I flew over to Talbots and plunked
down fifty dollars for a pair of conservative khakis. I wear the
pink pants less now. Think about pastoral situations, and take
a look at your wardrobe. The pink pants may have to wait for
Saturday. Another practical tip: if you wear a lapel or head-
set microphone, you may want to find clothes with pockets for
worship services, if you are not wearing a robe. While the male
head of staff finds it easy to go without a robe and stick his
microphone box in his pocket, my solution involves duct tape.

While I don't wear my pink pants much anymore, I am still
me—just a different version, a "robed" version. I have found
that the robe does give me some authority with some people,
especially those who grew up in the church, typically those who
always call me "Reverend" and never just "Marianne." I have
found that there are occasions when wearing a clergy shirt has
helped me minister to people I encounter in the community.
I have also found that wearing this clerical garb helps me to

don my internal "robe" and take on that pastoral identity. Yet with most people, my authority does not come from what I am wearing or what I look like at all, especially because what I look like is not the stereotypical picture of wisdom and power. My authority comes from the ministry I have worked among them and from the relationship I have with them. That relationship, that ministry—the sermon I preached that challenged their perspectives, the retreat I led that touched their hearts, the moment I stood beside them in a time of grief—that is the true "robe" I wear, the one God has woven around me, stitch by stitch, each day in God's service.

Finding Your Voice

Even though I believe that my ministry is flourishing and that I have grown into the role, every once in a while I have a reality check. I once visited an older woman and asked her what she liked about the church. She replied, "It's so nice to hear a man talk." I began to wonder how God could use me in that situation—or if I had better just pray and leave.

I am a soprano, and when I entered the ministry, I felt rather self-conscious about my voice. This feeling intensified when I listened to myself on a CD. Why couldn't I have a booming baritone, sounding a bit more like James Earl Jones? Why couldn't I sound more commanding and authoritative? Why couldn't I sound more like, well, God is supposed to sound? Must I sound so *squeaky?*

If preaching or worship leadership is a part of your ministry, you will have to encounter your own voice. The spoken word is a very important part of the worship service in most churches, as it should be. The book of John begins with the importance of the Word: "In the beginning was the Word, and the Word was with God, and the Word was God" (John 1:1). We encounter God primarily through words. Thus the words that we speak are of great importance. Indeed, our speech will help the congregation encounter God. The book of John also relates, "My sheep hear my voice, and I know them, and they follow me (John 10:27). If you are a young woman, your voice may not automatically help people encounter God, if they can hear only the voice of a male, or particularly an older male, as authoritative. It may even be difficult for some people to hear you, as many older people lose the ability to hear higher pitches as they age. Yet you are also able to help people literally to hear a fresh voice proclaiming God's Word.

As you work with sound systems while ministering week after week, you may literally find your voice in worship leadership. You may find it helpful to use a digital voice recorder to hear how you sound—for example, when I get excited about what I am saying, sometimes my voice gets higher and my speaking faster. Recording myself helps me to recognize which parts of the sermon I need to slow down and deepen. As with the other areas of embodied ministry, you will "wear a robe"— you will find that you have a worship voice, a robed voice. Since I began ministry, I have both accepted my voice and worked on my voice. I have a different, "robed" voice when leading worship. It actually sounds kind of funny in a nonworship context. It is deeper and slower than my speaking voice. It is the voice of proclamation. It is a voice that conveys that what is being spoken has great importance, that this young girl, like Mary singing her heart out, may even speak for God.

The Girlfriends' Checklist:

* Never forget that you are an embodied person. God called you to ministry just as you are. Be yourself.
* Remember Mary. God can use the openness and vulnerability of the young.
* Keep your sense of style, and allow your style to be a ministry to your congregation.

- As a young woman, recognize that it is more likely that people will notice, and comment on, your style and embodied self.
- Wear a "robe." Find a pastoral identity that works with your style and embodiedness, but remember that for most people, your authority comes from your ministry and relationship with them rather than from your appearance.
- Find your voice and speak God's Word.

·5·

Fight for Your Right to Party

SASSY AND SINGLE IN MINISTRY

Amanda Adams Riley

••••

S o you managed to escape seminary without an MRS degree to match your MDiv Congratulations. Now that you've been jettisoned from the warm nest of seminary with the common dining hall and lots of obvious peer groups, it's time to make friends on your own. So whether you are single and happy that way, or single and actively pursuing a partner, or in a long-term relationship but trying to have a life outside of love, this chapter is for you.

Let's begin by talking about how wonderful it is to be single. I have one word for you: independence. Being single, especially if you are living on your own (without roommates), can be liberating. It is nice to leave work and know that you can go anywhere and do anything and no one (a) knows or (b) cares. If you want to go on an impromptu shopping trip, go. If you want to go home and curl up on the couch with a good book, do it. If you want to have yogurt or Chinese takeout for dinner, no one is looking and no one cares. You can do whatever you want whenever you want. You are in charge of your life! Live it and love it, because if you do end up with a spouse one day, you will no longer enjoy the same kind of freedom. I remember one evening after some long meetings, I decided I couldn't wait any longer to decorate my apartment for Christmas, so I went to a twenty-four-hour store and bought some decorations. I then stayed up until 1:00 a.m. decorating with Christmas music blaring. It was wonderful! Being single is great! The freedom the single life affords you means that you can accept a ministerial call wherever you feel led without having to balance the expectations and desires of another. It means you can use your vacation time for anything you can dream up without feeling that it *has* to be used to strengthen your marriage or to visit in-laws. Being single comes with a lot of freedom that the married and partnered folks don't get to enjoy. (Now the obvious downside of being single is that it can be lonely. This is an issue for all clergy, one we address further in chapter 8, but single pastors may find the loneliness especially intense.)

As a pastor, you will find that people make many demands on your time, and as a single person you might find it's very hard to say no. Your colleagues who have spouses or children or both will have a plethora of reasons why they are unable to take part in certain events, including but not limited to their spouse, their children, their in-laws, their in-laws' children— the list goes on; all need something or have some other event that conflicts with the church event. You will not have as many obvious excuses, but you have just as much right to take time away from work as everyone else. Notice I said "take" time. You might feel as if you are taking time that may not belong to you. You'd be right: it doesn't belong to you (or the church); it belongs to God. We are all given time on this earth, and we do not know how much time we have, but what we do know is that we are to use that time for the glory of God and to enjoy God fully (paraphrased from the Westminster Confession). There are many ways we can glorify and enjoy God, and they do not all include our work in the life of the church.

You, like all ministers, have the right to take time for yourself. Taking time for yourself starts by making your personal time a high priority. You will have a day off; do everything you can to take it. When you know ahead of time that you have a work obligation on your usual day off, do your best to take off another day or parts of other days that week. Now, it can be hard to leave the office if you feel (or have been told) that you are expected to sit at your desk from 9:00 a.m. to 5:00 p.m. The main thing to remember is that your work will never be done. Serving a church is not like finishing a paper or reaching the end of the semester. There will always be more people to visit. There will always be a newsletter or a sermon to write or a program to work on. No matter how efficient you are, there will always be more to do, and sometimes you will just have to walk away. The work will be there tomorrow and next week; *just walk away.*

If you are good at saying no to all the extras that will be asked of you and leaving the office when you mean to, then you can stop reading here. But most of you will find that to have time for yourself, you either have to be very good at leaving the office when you intend too, or you have to be busy outside the church. Perhaps "being busy" means scheduling time to read, taking a walk, or doing something you enjoy and find rejuvenating. This approach works only if you can prevent that time from being scheduled over or bumped because of what seems like a pressing church obligation.

The best way I have found to strive for some kind of balance is to have a life outside church. This means pursuing activities and hobbies. It also means having friends, especially some outside the congregation. If you, like me, graduated from seminary with few hobbies, now is the time to get some! Before moving to your first call, take time to think about what you would like to do with your free time. Look into some activities that will both give you a reason to leave work and help you make friends. If you're eager to find a new hobby, see what other single people (who aren't necessarily clergy) are up to. Since seminary, I have developed friendships with people who are involved in everything from martial arts to learning to play a new instrument to drag racing. I have friends who have taken up (and, yes, these are all women) salsa dancing, sport fighting, boxing, and bodybuilding. Not really a jock? What about a cooking class, beekeeping, or pottery making? To find people to do your newfound hobby with, beyond the usual social networking websites, look for the websites that allow you to form groups around a common interest in your area and meet these individuals face to face. These sites have groups organized around everything from beagles to Monty Python.

Taking a day off in a rural setting can be tricky if you find yourself routinely doing pastoral care in the frozen-food section of the grocery store or getting phone calls at home for church business on your day off. It may be the case that the only way to have a true "day off," or sabbath, is to leave town. Use these opportunities to explore nearby areas. Look for an alumni group from your alma mater, or visit friends from seminary who are less than a day's drive away. For those who live in small towns and rural areas, forming friendships, especially with people your own age, will be a challenge, but it is not impossible. It's just unlikely that you will find another single clergyperson your age to be best friends with.

In my first call, I found friends through colleagues in the area, through the brother of a friend from high school (random, I know) who was living nearby, and through volunteer activities. I also recognized that I needed regular contact with people my own age. Knowing that one way to form a strong peer group is to see each other, I set up a "ladies night" and invited all the young women I knew who lived in the area and who were, or might become, good friends of mine. Entertaining may not be everyone's favorite activity and this may sound like work to some, but you don't have to host gatherings to organize them. Having several groups of friends (only one of which was tied to the church) helped encourage me to establish some boundaries about my time. And when asked on Sunday morning, "How was your weekend?" I had actual answers!

Depending on your denomination's or congregation's policies, you likely have between two and four weeks of vacation each year. Taking your allotted vacation time is important. Ministry is a taxing and an all-consuming call; therefore, it is essential for you and for your ministry to have real "quality time" away. Now there are obvious ways to use vacation. Visiting family is one. But unless you want to spend weeks with your family each year, you will probably need some other ways to use vacation. Vacation is a chance to spend time with friends, or to get away for a long weekend—the whole weekend, not just up to Saturday night. Go meet up with friends in a vacation area, plan a getaway with seminary classmates, or go on a shopping trip with girlfriends.

For those who have more vacation time than they know what to do with, here are some ideas about how to use your vacation. Get in the habit of taking your birthday off. Do not pass up the opportunity to spend time away with people of your choice and to do things that are important to you. When you are fresh out of school, the odds are that you are not like Scrooge McDuck swimming around in piles of money, so taking vacations may also require being cost-conscious. Staying with a friend is often the least expensive route, but you can also take vacation time when a friend comes to see you. If you are planning to visit a place where you don't know anyone, keep in mind that church-related conference centers and monasteries often offer small rooms for $35 to $50 per night. Want to fly? Discount ticket websites offer lots of deals and will even e-mail you price alerts. I recently heard of an airline that lets you fly anywhere in the country for one month straight for one price! You could take several weeks away all at once, and see Seattle and Miami in one month.

Assumptions and Expectations

I had the privilege of sitting in on a pastoral call committee during which there was a discussion about a candidate who was young and single, never married. I figured they would think that his being single would be an asset; no spouse or kids meant he would have more time to give to the church. Instead, I heard concerns about the nature of single men. One member of the committee said, "What if he's a party animal?" I was shocked. It did not even occur to me to wonder about the potential for a single pastor to be a "party animal" or even a "womanizer." After all, he's just a beginning pastor. Isn't he going to be too stressed about his sermons to party hard on Saturday night? Whether we like it or not, people have expectations, often based on assumptions about how we will behave as a result of our marital status.

In seminary I remember being told by a male classmate that one of his fears about leaving seminary without a wife or fiancée was that people might mistakenly think he was gay, and that he would face discrimination. This was certainly something that had never crossed my mind, and yet, the reality is that people make assumptions about every candidate depending on many factors, including gender, age, and marital status.

The assumptions made about us lead to expectations of our behavior. Knowing that there are and will be assumptions made about us and consequently expectations of our behavior helps us to navigate difficult situations. It is also important to note that what is acceptable behavior for a male colleague of our age and marital status may not be prudent for us. What's more, alcohol consumption can be a sticky issue for many congregations. Even for those who don't have any tradition of prohibiting alcohol use, there may be a regional component to churches' concerns about alcohol. For example, while it might be okay for our male counterparts to have a beer at a funeral reception, it might not be for us. If you are called to an associate position, the expectations others have of you and your behavior will be different from those people have for someone called to be "the" pastor. For example, it may be acceptable for the head of staff to have a glass of wine at dinner with minors present but not for the associate, because she works directly with children and youth. Some of my colleagues who work with youth, for example, have adopted a policy of not imbibing in the presence of youth, even if it is an adult function and everyone else has a glass of wine. Others don't drink alcohol or smoke at all in the presence of church members. Yet others I know believe it is imperative to level the playing field with congregation members by being "one of the guys" and having a beer. I know this issue has been a difficult one for me to navigate, because on the one hand, I don't want to seem "holier than thou," and yet I feel uncomfortable drinking with a group of congregation members, one of whom abstains. No matter what choice you make, it is important to remember that whether you like it or not, the congregation and the community have expectations of you as a pastor.

Now for the expectations of conduct that are specific to being single. We all need a place to cut loose, a place where we can be free to act our age, have a glass of wine, or—gasp!—wear a short skirt. Whether we like it or not, there is a difference between a single woman cutting loose and a married woman cutting loose. People expect that the husband or partner will take care of a woman if she gets too wild and crazy, but as single women we are considered riskier. A short skirt on a single woman makes more of a statement than the low-cut top on a woman with a rock on her finger. Eventually, weeks or years of being on your best behavior may give way to some . . . well, less-than-ideal moments. Most of my single clergy friends have a story of a time when they were away from their congregation and cut loose—a little too loose. Although none of these events caused repercussions for their careers, it's important to note that we all have the potential to cut "too loose."

Most of the stories involve a guy and drinks, and none involve any breaking of ordination vows, but most concern the kind of experience on which a person looks back and thinks, "Really? Is that what I did?" They are all the kinds of experiences we would regret a congregation member's having been privy to. The truth is that we all need space to have these wild-child moments, so whether you are a young clergyperson or simply young at heart, it is important to allow yourself a safe place to cut loose every once in a while. Not allowing yourself this space can lead to such moments arising in an unplanned and unwanted way.

"So What Do You Do?"

Your not-so-wild-child days might be behind you, and you've begun dating or are at least prepared for the opportunity. If you're like me, you were told in seminary not to date anyone in your congregation. If you choose to do this anyway (and many do), I recommend that you have a serious, concrete discussion—as unromantic as this sounds—with your "special friend" about the possibility of a breakup and what would happen if your relationship does not end well. There is a chance that one of you will want to leave the church. If you plan to go forward, it is wise to keep this relationship quiet, because all eyes are on you as a pastor and will be on your new partner. Should the relationship progress to discussions of marriage, it may be worth letting congregation members know slowly, depending on your situation. If you are in a small church or small town where everyone knows more or less everything about everyone else, then you may want to let the word spread before you announce your engagement. Unexpectedly showing up one day with a rock on your finger may hurt the feelings of those who are close to you and your partner. On the other hand, if you are in a larger congregation or a city and you don't want the members questioning you about the state of your personal relationship, you might wait until there is a formal commitment between you and your partner to break the news.

If you meet someone outside the church and begin to date, take some time to think about how the congregation might relate to him. If your congregation is small, the members may become attached to your significant other, and if things don't work out, the breakup may be difficult for everyone. My advice is to keep things quiet until the relationship has progressed to a point where you are seriously looking toward marriage in the near future.

Local and long-distance relationships might be introduced differently to the congregation, but do your best to take into account both your own rights to privacy and the possibility of the relationship's ending. Because you have probably lived in more than one area, you might as easily end up with an out-of-town significant other as an in-town one. These are really two different animals. They also behave differently, depending on the kind of community you are serving. For example, if you live in a manse or parsonage, then all eyes are certainly on you. If you live in a house near the church, and members drive by your house and are known to comment on whether you had a party recently—again, all eyes are on you. If you live nowhere near any other members and, say, in an apartment, then you may have tons of anonymity.

Let's look at the most complicated situation—the out-of-town boyfriend and the manse. In all likelihood, he is not independently wealthy and therefore not able to stay in a hotel every time, and he's unlikely to have a friend in town who has a couch he can crash on. Living in a manse, you will probably have a spare bedroom, and it would only be natural for him to stay there. Here's the rub—appearances. You know your congregation, and you know what members may or may not be comfortable with. Be aware of how your actions may be perceived by your congregation.

The in-town boyfriend will provide some challenges too. If you live in a small town, then going on dates in town may put you on display, as might any doorstep goodnights. Creativity will be key, as will open and honest talks. Whatever situation you are in, it is important to be aware of people's expectations of you, a religious public figure in your community.

If you start dating, you should know this: you are not the first and you will not be the last to date or be in a romantic relationship while serving a congregation. Although this may feel like uncharted territory (and it may be for you and the church you serve), you are not alone. Consider reaching out to colleagues and listening to their stories. You will find the best path through these murky waters, but it may take some time.

Depending on how open you are with your congregation about what you are doing every time you leave them, vacationing with your newfound love may be easy or complicated. My congregation did not ask a lot of questions about where I vacationed, so I was able to take several vacations with my future husband, including one to Paris, where he proposed. If you readily disclose vacation details to your congregation, you may have to start becoming more vague about your plans.

Let's consider the implications when you say yes to a marriage proposal. There are various ways to share this joyous news with the congregation. The most subtle is just letting people notice. The next would be announcing it in some forum, whether at a meeting of church leaders or as part of the sharing of "joys and concerns" during worship. There are many ways to spread the good news. Know your setting, and share the news in the most appropriate way to your setting. Big news travels fast, and your congregation will be happy for you. In all likelihood, members will throw a shower for you. Be prepared for lots of attention and love from the church.

Depending on their previous history with pastors and engagements, parishioners may be simply overjoyed. On the other hand, if the last pastor they had who got engaged used it as an exit strategy, you may experience a less-than-joyous response. As with all things, context matters. If you haven't already discussed this question with your new partner, now is the time to figure out how the love of your life relates to the congregation.

Will he enroll in the next new members' class, or remain active in his current house of worship, or simply stay home? However this may look, prepare your partner and yourself for the congregation's probing questions.

Now that you're engaged, the next questions will be about the wedding. I know of four potential models, none of which is perfect, but each of which has worked for a clergywoman.

Option 1: The out-of-town wedding. If your family is traditional and you plan to get married in your hometown, and that happens to be a long drive or plane flight from the church you are serving, then there is no need to worry about whether to invite congregation members. If for some reason they have not met your fiancé, however, then you may want to consider allowing them to host some kind of engagement party or wedding reception. In general, this is the neatest option for getting married while serving a church.

Option 2: The destination wedding. Like option one, this tends to be pretty clean cut, and a party of some sort before or after the wedding where the members can congratulate you and your new spouse may be expected. Be prepared for a shower or reception.

Option 3: The "in-town" or nearby wedding. If you met your spouse in town and planning a wedding far away stresses you out, then this may be the way to go. The easiest thing is to get married in the church you are serving, but if this gives you the heebie-jeebies, then perhaps something a few towns over will do nicely. That arrangement can both afford distance from the congregation and save you from having to find a florist four states away whom you will never meet and having to fly in early to file for the marriage license. If you get married in the church you are serving, it is wise to invite all the members to the wedding. This is pretty easy if you have just a ceremony, but once you add a meal and a cake, things can get pricey fast. You might have a cake-and-punch reception for everyone after the service at the church and then a more formal dinner if needed for family, close friends, and any other VIPs later that day. For a nearby wedding, you may be able to get away with not inviting all of the congregation (say, just staff) to the ceremony and reception. But a word to the wise: my husband and I tried this and ended up with a few party crashers, so be prepared.

Option 4: Getting married Sunday morning! While this may sound like a strange option, more than one clergyperson I know has chosen it. It allows the congregation to take part in the special day, and if you do end up marrying a member of the congregation, this plan may make the most sense. The rub comes when we begin thinking about the reception. As with the in-town or nearby wedding, it may be wise to have a cake-and-punch reception in lieu of coffee hour, so that everyone can celebrate with you and then, if needed, have a fuller evening or midafternoon reception for family and out-of-town guests.

Being single and serving a congregation has its blessings and its challenges. There will be times when loneliness creeps in. There will be times when you feel taken advantage of because of your marital status. And there will be times when you will feel blessed to have the flexibility that the single life allows. However your call and life take shape, remember to take time out to foster friendships and to take care of yourself, so you can continue shepherding the flock.

The Girlfriends' Checklist

- You can say no. The fact that you don't have the excuse of someone waiting at home doesn't mean you have to do every last little thing the church asks.
- Friends come first. Put life-giving relationships first, so that you will have energy to give to your call.
- Keep your private life private. That you are a semipublic figure doesn't mean that the congregation has a right to know whom you are dating and the progress of your relationship.
- Break the news of a marriage proposal well. Your congregation loves you, and this is an important time in your life. The members will want to support you; let them.

·6·

The Pastor's "Wife"
They Didn't Expect

YOU'RE NOT MARRIED TO THE CHURCH

Marianne J. Grano

• • • •

Since I became a married ordained woman, my husband and I have received mail addressed to the following:

Mr. and Mrs. Daniel Grano
Mr. Daniel and Mrs. Marianne Grano
Mr. Daniel and Rev. Marianne Grano
Rev. Marianne and Mr. Daniel Grano
Rev. and Mr. Marianne Grano

The variety of the names on invitations demonstrates a central fact of the clergywoman's marriage: there is no standard on how to treat it. Books of etiquette actually differ on the correct wording for such a couple, and the way in which an invitation or a place card reads will demonstrate to you the attitude of a host or hostess toward women in ministry and relationships. You can do something about the wording in some instances, by being clear about, for instance, how your names appear on mailing lists or in directories. But the reality that you will never be able to control how people choose to address you underscores the deeper reality that you will never be able to control how other people might react to your situation as a married or partnered clergywoman. Some will expect your partner to play the traditional role of the pastor's spouse, as an active member of the church, present every Sunday, and central to the life of the church you are serving. Others might expect your spouse to play the role of a modern spouse with a separate career. The type of ministry you are in will affect the expectations that people have, and the situation of a clergy couple in different churches or serving as copastors creates its own expectations. You must clearly determine what role your spouse will play in your community life and your congregational life. You must answer for yourself and your spouse the question, how will your relationship work with your ministry? With all the expectations around you, you must determine what is best for your relationship. These issues can be tricky for all clergy in relationships—young, female, or otherwise—and I hope this chapter will be helpful to any married minister.

I believe that your marriage will be at its healthiest if you are one another's support system first and foremost. Your spouse is the person you will call first when your new ministry fails. Your spouse is the one with whom you can share your dreams for a future call. You may find yourself talking about church with your spouse and gaining perspective that you would not get from other staff or congregation members. The support of someone who loves you is invaluable to your ministry. Yet I believe your marriage, not your ministry, ought to come first.

When I was in seminary, one professor asked us whether we would rather be better pastors than spouses or better spouses than pastors. We all said we would rather be better spouses than pastors. You are accountable to God for your ministry, but you are also accountable to God for the way that you love the person God has given you to love. You must remember this always, or your marriage will be drowned in the sea of church life.

As the Presbyterian Church (U.S.A.), other denominations, and our society at large debate issues of marriage and lesbian, gay, bisexual, and transgendered (LGBT) relationships, we are constantly reminded that it is difficult for the church to talk about intimate relationships. We authors are all married to men. Although I will continue to use the term "spouse," a person in an unmarried heterosexual relationship or a lesbian relationship would face these issues too. I will also talk about marriage and husbands because that is the authors' frame of reference. Also, I will mostly address the situation of parish ministry, although I think these issues would carry into other forms of ministry.

Keeping Your Boundaries Clear

As young women clergy, some of us influenced by third-wave feminism, we are proving more likely to marry than the previous generation. Yet we have a particular set of baggage to deal with that women doctors and lawyers are unlikely to face: the role of the pastor's spouse. In interviews, I was often questioned extensively as to the role my future husband would play and whether he would join the church I would serve. Because of my husband's work situation, I was geographically bound, and I was going to have to be a commuter pastor, which was a dealbreaker for some churches. I sometimes felt as though what the churches really wanted was a young man with a wife who was a full-time mom or who had an easily transportable job.

Listen closely during the interview process to any comments about spouses. Churches have an institutional memory—they have patterns, healthy or unhealthy, that they have followed for years or decades. Some churches have a healthy respect for the boundaries of a marriage. Others do not. Find out what role the previous pastor's spouse held in the church. If you're interviewing for an associate position, find out about the role of the head pastor's spouse. Pay attention to any questions a search committee asks about your spouse.

When I found the right church, part of what made me sure I was called was the way in which church people dealt with my husband. One woman on the search committee asked about my engagement ring and then congratulated me with a big smile. Other than that, there was no discussion of my spouse. I felt, from that brief exchange, that the committee was supportive of me and my relationship but did not need my fiancé to fill a specific role. Other committees I met with asked many more questions about my fiancé, and that made me uncomfortable.

The good news is that because you will never truly fit into the traditional model of a pastor and pastor's wife, you have options! Your spouse could be peripherally involved in your church or of another belief system. Your spouse could be involved in another church. Your spouse could be highly involved in your church. Your spouse might be your copastor. Some of these options might be harder in one church than another. For this reason, you should determine what role individuals in your church, and the congregation as a whole, expect your spouse to play. Then you must work on communicating the role your spouse will actually play and setting appropriate boundaries in your congregation.

There will be people who don't understand that your partner's primary role is to be your partner. If your spouse is not actively involved in your ministry, there will be people who ask why. If your spouse is actively involved in your ministry, people may not understand that there are still boundaries—they can't give a document to your spouse and expect you to get it. They can't call the house and tell your husband something that needs to be communicated directly to you. Boundaries have to be constantly maintained, and you can't expect anyone to maintain them except the two of you.

When He Doesn't Go to Church

Some young clergywomen I have known have a husband who is not of the same faith or does not attend her church. Your husband might not have a problem with Christianity but still not be a big churchgoer. Or your husband may not be a Christian. One woman I know whose husband wavers between agnosticism and atheism finds that it is difficult for him to understand some of the spiritual issues with which she deals. Martin Copenhaver writes on the struggles of a minister in his chapter "Married to a Pagan" in *This Odd and Wondrous Calling*, coauthored with Lillian Daniel. A congregation would have to be trained to understand such a situation, and it's best if you as pastor work out in advance how you will communicate your situation to the congregation. People in the church may not be able to understand why he doesn't go to church as easily as your friends in seminary understood it. You yourself will also have to deal constantly with your spouse's not fully believing in something so important to you and your life's work. You have to mourn that loss and make peace with it.

Yet in another way, it may be very easy for you to allow your partner just to be your partner and support *you*. You married this person because of love, and you promised to be faithful in good times and bad. You have access to a fresh perspective from someone outside the church on what is going on in the Christian community. Savor that gift. You also have an escape from church life and an opportunity to explore other interests together. You will always know that your partner is not there to be the "pastor's wife," the unpaid church staff. Your partner's role is clearly to support you.

As a woman in ministry, you may find it easier than a man would for your spouse not to be involved in the church, because there is less expectation that your husband function as an unpaid staff person than there might be of a traditional pastor's wife. Yet you will have to deal with questions like, "How can you be a good role model for the youth of the church when your husband doesn't even go to church?" Or you might be compared to the previous pastor: "Pastor Doug's wife, Alice, always cooked for the pancake breakfast." You have two distinct and separate callings in your life: being a pastor and being a wife. God called you to both of them. Hold onto that, don't be defensive, and protect your relationship first and foremost.

When He Always Goes to Church

In seminary I knew some men who were looking for a pastor's wife. There are still women out there who feel called to be the "first lady" of the church. You may have the gift of a husband who wants to be "first gentleman" of the church, who wants to play an active role in your ministry. That's quite a gift! Don't take it for granted!

If your spouse is highly involved in your church, you will have a lot of joys to share together. You will have many shared experiences. However, I believe that you should set some boundaries on where the church begins and ends. While I personally do not know any women clergy who are copastors with their husbands, I would guess that boundaries are important in that situation too. If you are serving as copastors or both highly involved in the same church, remember that your ministries need individual time and attention. Take time to be supportive of one another as individuals in ministry and as individuals who have a life outside ministry. If he is a layperson, give him appreciation as you would another layperson. If he is a copastor, support his ministry as you would if he were not your spouse.

Practically, it becomes very important to communicate several boundaries to the church. For example, if people call one of you and ask you to direct information to the other, it's up to you to say, "Sorry. You'll need to call back after six, or you can leave a message on his voicemail at work. Do you have that number?" After a while, most folks will figure it out—but it's always up to you to say no. If you don't draw this boundary, you are setting yourself up to have many miscommunications, or to spend your evenings relaying information related to the church.

Another important boundary is setting aside time for non-church activities. Plan vacations to do interesting things together. Spend time doing things that have nothing to do with the church. Find a TV program you both like that you can share. Get involved in a nonprofit together. Enjoy the outdoors. When you realize you've spent an entire dinner talking about the church, *stop*. The church cannot be the only bond between you. Your marriage and family need space.

Part of keeping your marriage and family sacred is learning that you can say no to some things. It's important, too, that you develop church leadership. People may rely on the two of you, as the "mom and dad" of the church, to do everything. What happens when, someday, you leave? You need to say no sometimes for the health of the church as well as for the health of your marriage and yourselves as individuals.

When He Goes to Church Sometimes

My husband is highly involved as a layperson in the church where both of us grew up, which is in the metro area where we live and work. He is an elder, a youth leader, and a delegate to our presbytery. I am an associate pastor and youth director in another church. It is difficult for some people in our lives to understand why my husband doesn't go on my mission trips or confirmation retreats and goes on his own mission trips and confirmation retreats. Sometimes it's hard for *me* to understand. Our session meetings are on different nights. Our confirmation retreats are on different weekends. Our mission trips couldn't even be scheduled at the same time, so basically we aren't seeing each other this June. But there are several very good reasons why we are doing it this way. Dan was already very active in that church when I took my call. It is *his church*, and it is difficult for a person who loves his church to change churches. Our whole family attends that church. His calling as a layperson in that church is something I have to respect.

Also, he has made it clear that I can't be his pastor. We are too close—basically, he knows that I'm not holy! When we have tried having him serve as an adult leader in my church, the biggest problem is that he misses having me as a wife. Because I'm working, I can't give him the attention and affection he is used to. He has trouble coming to church events, because I can't just sit and enjoy them with him. I am constantly interacting with members of the congregation. For us, it does not work. What does work for us is his coming to my church when I preach and on high holidays, my coming to his church when I have time off, and both of us being part of the communities and the presbytery together. Although I am often asked, "Why isn't Dan here?" *it doesn't have to work for my congregation; it has to work for Dan and me.* There are plenty of people who should step forward in the church without my needing to recruit family members.

If your husband comes to church sometimes, he is giving you the gift of treating your ministry like any other job—where there is time on and time off. He is acknowledging that he should support you, but also stating that there are limits on that support. You can learn from this. The church can be part of your life, without being the whole.

Some Practical Suggestions

Being married and in ministry is largely a question of good stewardship of time. If your spouse is not in ordained ministry, the times he has off may be different from the times you have off. In the parish, Sunday is often the biggest workday, and evenings are busier than mornings. You and your spouse may not have a weekend together. Christmas and Easter are no longer breaks for you. You will have to carve out time to be together. If, like many young clergywomen, you are just beginning a marriage, it is good for you to establish a pattern or system from the beginning. Because we have so many evening and weekend commitments, Dan and I have a couple's calendar in the kitchen. Any evening or weekend event is written on the calendar. That way, we can plan when we will have dinner together or, miraculously, an entire day. An even better system would be to schedule the "couple time" first so that we don't just get the "leftovers." Keeping the calendar helps us notice when commitments should be moved to a different day or time so that the scheduled "dates" can remain intact. Now that we have a daughter, it also helps us figure out when we need to arrange for child care! You need to decide what is the least amount of time together you will accept as a couple. If there comes a week when you simply can't have three dinners together, what else will you say no to the next week so that you *can* have enough time together?

Along with the couple's calendar, an important principle of our life is the sacredness of the day off. I had a conversation with a pastor's wife in her eighties, and she told me to never, never let work creep into your day off. When her husband began working on his day off, their marriage began to deteriorate, and he ended up having an affair with a woman in the church. If you are a good steward of time at the church, you should be able to disconnect from the church one day a week, except for pastoral emergencies. I do not check my e-mail on my day off. If I did, I would end up working for an hour or more. People know how to reach me if there is a pastoral emergency that no one else can handle. I try not to let the day off become totally swamped by housework and child care, and to take some time for myself and my husband.

His Life Matters Too!

Supporting one another takes planning and intentionality. If you are going to really be a support system for each other, you also have to respect your partner's limits. He may not want to hear your sermons before you preach them. He may not want to talk about church for the whole dinner hour. He may actually have a career that is as important and interesting as yours—and even if it's not, it's still a part of his life. Dan's career has been an enormous gift to me. He is an attorney who deals with people and situations far off my radar screen. His firm includes people of many different faiths and of no faith, and his clients and legal situations involve an entire different world. As his wife I am called to support him emotionally through all of his world, just as he supports me through all of mine. I am called to recognize the importance of what he is doing—to ask questions and to care about the answers. And it's a great, healthy outlet for me to be able to be the lawyer's wife and to go to the Christmas party or out with his friends and colleagues who don't regularly interact with any church people. They always have great questions for me about ministry, but I don't feel obligated to represent my denomination or Christianity. It is healthy to recognize that there are plenty of people out there who don't know or care much about the Bible or theology or the church. I have decided that I can use his world as a place to just be me and enjoy myself.

At the same time, being a pastor and a woman means that there is a difference in how I relate myself to his career. Going back to the name game—my husband is politically active, and once, on a piece of campaign literature, we were referred to as "Mr. and Mrs. Daniel Grano." I gave him quite a little sermon that day on who I am and how I am to be referred to. On that piece of campaign literature, I was being put forward as a "first lady" in a way. That is a role I do not have the time or energy to play in the way that Dan may have wanted me to. Also, I am a called and installed pastor, and I prefer to be referred to as "Rev." rather than "Mrs." when I'm addressed formally. It was a good exercise in recognizing that we each define me and our relationship in a certain way. Since you are part of a couple as well as a woman in ministry, the two of you will need to make that definition and determine what works for you. It may be different in different circumstances—you may be "Rev." at certain times and "Mrs." at other times. He may sometimes be Mr. Daniel Grano, attorney, sometimes, and Mr. Marianne Grano, the pastor's husband, at others. There were a few conversations that I am really glad we had before we got married—for example, the day he told me he did not want me to be his pastor. There are also a few things I wish I had communicated better—for example, that in no circumstances do I want to be "Mrs. Daniel Grano" and that I cannot be the quintessential politician's wife. Have conversations about the roles you will play in one another's lives. Have conversations about how you will communicate those roles to the church.

As a couple, you need to find places outside the church where you can be together and enjoy yourselves and one another. One of those places can be your spouse's career. Find what works for both of you.

Love Is Its Own Ministry

At the end of the day, the issue before the married clergyperson is love. You may love your congregation and your ministry, but I believe *you need to love your spouse more*. And your congregation may love you, but I believe *your spouse needs to love you more*. Love is a great gift to your life and your ministry. But love also needs space, time, and energy. Love needs to be its *own* ministry.

Just as you were called to ordained ministry, you were called to love. Just as being in ministry redefines you, so does love. Just as being in ministry changes the way you refer to yourself, so does love. Just as being in ministry demands far more than forty hours a week and you're never really "off," so it is with love. Just as being in ministry is the way you serve God, so is love! Recognize that you can serve God by serving your marraige,

and you will find that your other ministry does not suffer for
it, but grows, because when you know you are rooted in love,
you can thrive.

The Girlfriends' Checklist

- Keep in mind that there is no standard way to treat the
  clergywoman's spouse—you have options!
- Remember that the primary role of your spouse as related to your ministry is to be your spouse; you are one
  another's support system.
- Intentionally carve out time together as a couple. Establish a system like a couple's calendar. Keep your day
  off sacred.
- Find interests outside the church you can enjoy and talk
  about together. If your spouse is not working in ministry, his workplace can be a great gift to you.
- Remember that love is its own ministry. You may love
  the church, but you love your spouse more, and you are
  accountable to God for the ministry of your love.

·7·

Married . . . with PKs

MATERNITY LEAVE AND MOTHERING IN MINISTRY

Melissa Lynn DeRosia

••••

A colleague asked me once which day I took off each
week.

I laughed.

I laughed hard.

Day off? How, as a pastor, mother, and wife, would you define a day off? Is it the day that I don't check my e-mail? take
pastoral calls? talk with the parishioner who stops by to chat?
put the finishing touches on my sermon? Or the day I don't
wash the floors, clean bathrooms, or fold laundry? Maybe a day
off is one when I am not constantly filling juice cups, changing
diapers (there might be a correlation there), and kissing make-
believe boo-boos.

I know that most mothers, whether they stay at home with
their children full-time or work outside the home part-time, are
faced with an incredible challenge to coordinate self-care with
the many responsibilities before them. The women I know are
remarkable beings, capable of doing multiple things at once. As

a woman and a pastor, I have the ability to nourish a child and a family of faith, sometimes concurrently. But to answer the question of my colleague without laughing (or crying): I don't get a day off.

Baby Vacation

My capacities to be a mother and to be a pastor were realized at the same time: I was seven months pregnant when I preached my first sermon at my first call as a pastor. When I accepted the call, I was already four months pregnant, though not yet showing. That fact was a powerful motivator to talk with the search committees about the terms of my call—in particular, parental leave. Technically, none of the committee members could ask me if I was pregnant (though a few of the ladies swear to this day that they knew). I thought I had to be the initiator in this conversation. Before sitting down with them, I did my homework. I called other pastor friends of mine to find out if maternity leave was included in their terms of call, took note of higher church governing bodies that set requirements for congregations, and even glanced at the Family Medical Leave Act (FMLA), though congregations are not subject to those regulations.

This church had never before offered "maternity leave" because, up to this point, its ministers had been male. The ministers' wives had had babies, and the congregation's only role had been to delight in supporting the family and the new baby. Not offering parental leave meant the church didn't have to think about filling the pulpit on Sundays, even if the minister spent a little more time at home with his wife and newborn.

The search committee members asked a lot of questions about my situation, because they weren't sure whether I had to serve the congregation a certain length of time before I could take such leave, and whether they wanted me to use my vacation time before maternity leave would kick in. Somewhat predictably, the search committee initially proposed a "business" model that included taking unpaid leave or filing for medical disability, rather than creating a model of caring for pastors and their families.

The matter was left unresolved until the congregation officially extended the call to me. Then I told the committee members that my husband and I expected the arrival of our first child in early April, and I presented them with a choice. I asked whether they would prefer that I start serving the congregation on January 1 and take maternity leave in April, or begin June 1 and be ready to work without the interruption of a leave. It turned out they were eager to have a pastor in place and were excited to welcome a new baby into the life of the congregation. That excitement motivated the search committee to include in the terms of my call a six-week maternity leave following the birth of a child.

My reasons for establishing maternity leave were by no means typical. Not every woman pastor is going to feel an urgent need to discuss maternity leave because she is six months pregnant. Still, I encourage all pastors (yes, men, too) to work with a nominating committee or a personnel committee to establish a parental leave for all pastors of the congregation. Even if you have chosen not to have children, don't think you will start your family while serving in this call, or have decided not to have any more children, initiating these policies helps create an atmosphere in which it is expected that the pastor will take the time needed to attend to the physical, emotional, and spiritual transitions of welcoming a new member of the family.

My Body, My Baby

My daughter was born three months and seven days after I started ministry in the parish. The congregation and I barely had time to build a relationship with one another before members were exposed to details of my life that made a few of them and me uncomfortable. In those first few months of my first call, I was *very* pregnant—not just the cute-little-belly pregnant, but the waddle-around-and-try-not-to-knock-anyone-over kind of pregnant. My being pregnant was not something that could be ignored, but some members were particularly audacious in their comments. I especially enjoyed one elderly woman whose nature was to speak her mind freely. As I was getting ready to leave her home one afternoon after a pastoral visit, I stood up from the table. She looked me up and down, patted my cheek, and said, "Oh, honey, you really are filling out with that baby weight, aren't you?"

Did my parishioner just call me fat? I was pretty sure she did. I smiled politely, trying not to let the hormones get the best of me, because who knows whether I would have laughed, cried, or started calling her names! Since that day, I have heard running commentaries on my weight, the swelling of my breasts (and their subsequent reduction), the size of my children, and their eating habits, development, and behaviors. Apparently, having one hour to sit and look at my body invites these kinds of comments (insert sarcasm here).

After my daughter was born, another uncomfortable detail that I as mother and pastor now had to navigate was whether to breastfeed my child at church. Like many mothers, I struggled with the trial and error of learning my child's idiosyncrasies, how my own body worked, and what to do with a screaming, hungry child when she was with me at church.

In the first few months, I tirelessly tried to get my first child on a schedule that worked around meetings, fellowship events, and worship. Right before worship I would try to get her to nurse and empty my breasts to prevent any leakage as I held the communion elements above the table. I couldn't seem to get this little life to understand how lucky she was to have a mom who worked as a pastor and had the "flexibility" to bring her to work and nurse her without depending on bottles of formula.

She didn't want to conform her schedule to mine and was quick to remind me that in this relationship, she was the boss.

To accommodate my child's on-demand feeding schedule, I at first tried to excuse myself whenever she needed to eat. I put up a sign on my office door in the church that read "Knock, please," and I locked the door. More and more I found myself behind this locked door and wondered if there wasn't another way. Of course, giving her a bottle would have been the most logical solution. It wasn't that I was opposed to a bottle, but for some reason my daughter was. She wanted her mommy, and so did everyone on the other side of that locked door.

I started wondering why I was hiding every time I needed to nurse my child. Laws were being passed in states all across this country to protect a woman's right to nurse her child in public. "Nurse-ins" were organized to gather groups of nursing moms with infants and toddlers in tow, who go to a place where a nursing mother has been shamed or verbally assaulted and stage a massive breastfeeding frenzy. To my knowledge there has never been a "nurse-in" at a church, but I wasn't looking to stage a protest. I just wanted to be able feed my child and carry on a conversation. So I did. It took a lot of practice, and more than once I got strange looks as I covered myself with a blanket and nourished the life that was hungry, impatient, and longing for the closeness and comfort of a mother's breast. But we made it work.

On the Front Line

Nursing my children at church is one example of the unusual boundaries between being a pastor and being a mom that I have had to navigate. Another has been trying to figure out who is going to take care of my children. In my first call I hoped that after maternity leave, I would be able to take advantage of a built-in benefit —the fact that my office was located in the parsonage (or manse) right next door to the church. A narrow sidewalk separated the two. When I was describing the proximity to a colleague who asked, "How close?" I irreverently responded, "So close you can spit from the house and hit the church."

That office has two doors—one to the outside and another that closes it off to the rest of the house. But my office was in the house—where my kids lived, played, ate, and generally had the run of things. If you had walked into my office and looked at my desk, you would have seen my computer, biblical commentaries, half a cup of cold coffee from earlier that morning, a sippy cup of apple juice, and chewed-on crayons. The last two items usually weren't mine.

In the first few years of their lives, my children spent a lot of time with me in my office. The arrangement my husband and I worked out was that after he left for work in the morning around 7:30 a.m., the girls would "hang out" with me until my mom (who lived nearby) or the woman we hired to care for our children, arrived at 10:00 a.m. "Hang out" is a term I use loosely. Usually they were hanging all over me while I was trying to get caught up on e-mails, work on my sermon, put together the bulletin, and write articles for the newsletter. The TV was on in the living room (right around the corner from my office). Age-appropriate cartoons blared from it, but the children paid little attention. Toys exploded from all corners of the house, but for some reason my computer mouse was the thing they wanted to play with. Exegeting was interrupted by potty breaks, and I couldn't write worship liturgy without one of them hitting, kicking, biting, or pushing, requiring time-outs or tearful hugs and apologies. This was my day. Other moms who are pastors invite this kind of chaos in the church by bringing their children with them to the office.

Making this kind of arrangement for "mommying" and ministering takes a lot of allies. For me, my first line of defense is my husband. I rely on him to make it home by dinnertime every night, so that I can get something done after we eat, while he is wrestling the troops into the bathtub. He is also home on weekends, a big plus. Most important, he is my partner, who cares for me when I feel overwhelmed from trying to pull off being both a mom and a minister.

The next line of defense is reliable and trustworthy child care. For me it was initially a combination of my mom and someone we hired to come to our home and care for our children. They did more than just take care of the children. They also washed the dishes, cleaned up after the kids, and kept up on laundry that would have otherwise piled up. As the girls got older, my husband and I made the decision to move them to a day-care center that accommodated our part-time needs and allowed us to pay by the hour rather than by the week.

Having these support systems in place has made all the difference for me, enabling me to remain on the front lines of ministry and motherhood. I am grateful for a wonderful partner, an extended family, and a congregation that gracefully allowed me to plot a course through this unfamiliar territory. I have wondered what it would be like not to have these support systems. A lot of ministry happens when day care isn't open. What do single moms in ministry do when there is an evening meeting and the church can't afford to bring in child-care providers to watch the pastor's kid? I recognize that this is a struggle not only for a pastor but also for many parishioners who want to give their time and energy to the church but can't afford or find care for their children. There aren't any easy answers for this situation. My hope is that as more and more women serve as pastors in our churches, congregations will be willing to have the conversations about how to meet the changing needs of *all* families.

Drenched in Community

The fact that I serve as the pastor of a church doesn't mean that I expect the congregation instantly to relinquish patterns established when it had only male pastors with wives who stayed at home and took care of the children and to adopt new and creative ways of embracing women pastors who integrate pregnancy, and subsequently their children, into ministry. Except, *I do*. I *do* expect our congregations to change their assumptions that "children should be seen and not heard" for the very reason that they promised to guide and nurture my children—and not just my children, but all children. In the Presbyterian Church (U.S.A.), before the water falls on the head of the person being baptized, the pastor turns to the congregation and asks: "Do you as members of the church of Jesus Christ promise to guide and nurture (*insert name here*) by word and deed, with love and prayer, encouraging them to know and follow Christ and to be faithful members of his church?" I believe that one of the ways a congregation fulfills its promise is to welcome children.

Welcoming children is a plus not only for the children and their families. Having my children be such an active part of my ministry means that the congregation has benefited as well. When I came to the first congregation I served, there were only one or two other very young children in the congregation, and many of the older members had forgotten what it sounded like to have active children in worship. Self-conscious about the noises, cries, and screeches of delight that escaped from my little ones' mouths, at first I worried that they would disrupt the meditative aspects of worship. Then I watched the smiles creep across people's faces when my child made a noise. I realized that their noises bothered me a lot more than they bothered the people in the pews.

It is because of my integration of mothering and ministry that I understand the impact of a child-friendly worship experience. Recognizing that young children have trouble sitting through an hour of worship without having anything to do, we dragged a small table up from the basement to the sanctuary, put it up behind a back pew, and placed coloring books, crayons, puzzles, and other "quiet" toys on it. Children were welcome to get up at any time and move to the table to play. I am always amazed at the number of children who sat back there and remembered more of the sermon than their parents did!

Because I was pastor of this congregation and my children were at the church so often, welcoming spaces for children were created, not just in the sanctuary but all over the church. In our fellowship area we had a pile of toys and games, places to color, and spills on the carpet. Okay, so maybe all this "welcoming space" wasn't provided so much for others as it was for my own kids, and others benefited from it. Either way, my kids came with me to worship, to social events, and from time to time even to meetings in the church. To my children the church building was an ordinary part of their daily lives. We lived right next door, and the church basement became our indoor playground in the winter, the communion table was a great place to hide, and leftover communion juice might even find its way into a sippy cup.

Be forewarned that this familiarity with "sacred space" can have its downside. There is such a thing as children having too much comfort, especially in those moments when you are serving as pastor and can't always see what is going on with your own children. A particular children's sermon comes to mind. The children of the church were gathered on the chancel steps listening to a story. My two-year-old daughter was seated on the edge of the group. I turned my eyes to read a page of the story to the group of captivated children, and suddenly I heard a chuckle escape from the congregation. I smiled, thinking how wonderful it was that the adults were enjoying the book, too, and then the chuckle became a full-blown laugh. I looked to my right and my left for the source of amusement, and before I could turn all the way around, a perfectly cubed piece of white bread landed in my lap. My child was tossing the body of Christ like T-shirts at a sporting event! She gave new meaning to the notion of "sharing" this meal, and it has taken me a long time to be able to give a children's sermon without my eyes being glued to my children.

Not every congregation is going to be as receptive to your exploring your role as pastor and mother in such an integrated way. Some will demand more separation and insist that when you are at church, you are pastor first and mom second. Another minister mom shared with me that someone from the "staff relations committee" (read: someone on the committee or someone on the committee speaking on behalf of someone in the congregation) asked her head of staff to "have a talk with her" about her child sitting up front with her in worship on the Sunday after Christmas. Yes, on one Sunday out of the entire church year, her husband had a last-minute, unexpected work engagement, there was no Sunday school because only her child and one other were in attendance, and she let her son sit on her lap in worship while someone else preached the sermon and she led the rest of worship. She thought it wasn't a problem, especially since the most traditional and regal church matriarch had commented to her on the way out, "That just reminded me of Mary and the baby Jesus. It was so beautiful." After trying to persuade her almost five-year-old child to sit and be still for an hour, she had a different image in mind. Still, she said, he wasn't horribly disruptive, and it's not as though it happened every week. As a pastor and mom who has been in this situation, I can imagine that for the "staff relations committee" to ask her boss to "have a talk with her" seemed to her like an attack on her parenting and professional roles. Obviously, that person from the "staff relations committee" needed a reminder about those baptismal vows to "guide and nurture." Perhaps, then, committee members would have seen my colleague's distress about what to do with her child during worship and would have invited the child to sit with them.

Despite these kinds of situations we "minister moms" deal with, I find that an overwhelming amount of love is shared with my children and me. The congregation where I served was literally the group that said, "We do," as they promised to guide and nurture my children. In word and deed, with love and prayer, members of the church community saw and interacted with my children more than with any other children in the congregation, because they were at the church more than the others. Some members of the congregation did take these baptismal vows seriously, a little too seriously at times.

Because members of the congregation spent so much time with me and my children, they took on the role of "surrogate grandparents" and at times treated me like their child and my children like their grandchildren. This role included sharing a wealth of advice and criticism about my parenting skills. On more than one occasion I heard a tongue clicked in disapproval, followed by a question like "Oh, Melissa, where is that child's hat?" Or after I gave my daughter three suckers in a row to help keep her quiet during a meeting, a church member inquired, "Is that much sugar good for her teeth?" I wanted to bite back, "They are baby teeth and will fall out anyway," but I held my tongue, recognizing that a defense of my parenting style is not always conducive to my role as pastor.

Your Mom Is a What?

I also recognize that my life as a pastor is not always conducive to my role as a parent. My children are still young—young enough that none of their friends have ever asked them to explain what their mommy does for her job. They are young enough that no one has ever told them that I can't be a pastor because I am a woman. Right now all they know is that sometimes they don't like God or the church because both take up time they would like me to spend with them. I don't spend a lot of time obsessing about it, but I do worry that my being a mother and a pastor will have a negative effect on their spiritual lives. They may grow up resenting the church and rejecting God. Or they may grow up feeling that the church will always be a community they can turn to for nurture and support to be the beloved children of God I believe them to be. I am holding out for the latter.

The Girlfriends' Checklist

- When negotiating terms of call, be sure to include parental leave.
- Be prepared for the helpful, wacky, and completely out-of-line things your parishioners will say to you once you are pregnant and have children.
- Discuss with your partner the child-care options that work best for your ministry context. And don't be afraid to revisit the conversation if things aren't working. You, your children, and all of your needs change over time.

·8·

You May Be a Master of Divinity, But You Are Not Superwoman

SELF-CARE AND THE YOUNG CLERGYWOMAN

Amanda Adams Riley

••••

When you are fresh out of seminary, you have more ideas and more energy than any other pastor you will meet, and that is a gift. Here's the downside of that gift: if you don't remind yourself that you hope to be at this work for forty years, then you might just run yourself into the ground. Don't do that. The number of fresh-out-of-seminary clergy who leave the ministry altogether within the first ten years is estimated at 50 percent.[1] Don't be that statistic. Want to know how? Keep reading.

Have a Life Outside Church

The life of a clergyperson can be isolating, and isolation can lead to loneliness. One reality is not talked about enough, however: ours is a unique calling. Its unique nature means that although we can do a variety of interesting and exciting things as part of our call, few people in the world understand what our position, with its privileges and responsibilities, is like. One way to stave off loneliness is to find friends. Clergy friends are more likely to understand where you are coming from and to share in your struggles in life and ministry. Nonclergy friends will give you an outlet into the normal world and allow you to get outside the walls of the church, and they may even help you be a better pastor. However you choose to find them, friends are essential to longevity in ministry.

I took my first call in Ann Arbor, Michigan. I had never been to Michigan, and I knew nothing about Michigan and no one who lived in Michigan. But like most recent seminary grads, I was eager to follow God's call to the ends of the earth. In my case, the end was a peninsula surrounded by the Great Lakes.

I remember a phone conversation with a friend from high school who, hearing where I was headed after seminary, said, "Oh, my brother lives there." "That's nice," I thought. Next, she said, "He has a great group of friends." Friends! Yes, please, that is what I will need in my first call—friends who are not church members! Sign me up! That was my first connection, my lifeline, my way of having a life outside the walls of the church and outside simply being clergy. My first call was quite unusual because I was part of a "Transitions into Ministry" program funded by the Lilly Endowment, which meant that I was plopped down into a large congregation along with two other new seminary grads, one of whom happened to be from my seminary. Others serving in my congregation at the same time included a campus minister, a young clergyman who had graduated from my seminary the year before I did, along with a twenty-something youth director and a thirty-something woman pastor with two young children. The Lilly Program afforded me built-in collegial relationships, some of which blossomed into friendships that I cherish to this day.

I came to my first call not expecting any of the built-in camaraderie and support of colleagues. I expected that I would need to forge my own relationships. So before even moving to the community, I began to lay groundwork for my hobby, volunteering. I looked up a few organizations that might provide an outlet for me. The first on which I settled was the local nonprofit hospice. I had been a hospice volunteer in college, and I knew the city was big enough that I would not necessarily be a hospice volunteer for members of my own congregation. At the volunteer training, I met a graduate student with whom I became friends. She became my one in-town, nonchurch friend.

I also joined a gym and signed up for yoga, so I could begin making friends through the outlet of recreation. At one point, I even played in an adult kickball league! Not my forte, I admit, but still—if you can dream it, there is probably an activity out there for you and a way for you to meet and make friends.

Another built-in outlet for those of us in connectional denominations (meaning our churches are not exclusively congregational) are regional gatherings of clergy (sometimes with laypeople), such as presbyteries, dioceses, or conferences. In fact, the genesis of this book came from relationships with other clergy in the same stage of life as I. One of my mentors in ministry also sought out a group of young clergywomen in her first years in the ministry. It is helpful to find peers in ministry, whether they are close to you in age, years in ministry, relationship status (single, married, married with kids), or simply serving in a comparable role (also an associate or also a solo in an urban church). They may not be nearby, but making the connection and fostering a relationship is worth the effort! Very few people in this world understand the complexities and blessings that come with our life.

If getting to know the clergy in your denomination doesn't work for you (because they are too far away, or simply not interested in being friend candidates for you), there may be some clergy in your city who could potentially become your friends. My town's area clergy organization has provided an outlet for me to meet other clergy and commiserate about the challenges of ministering in this community. Just the other day my husband said to one of the other pastors in town, who with his wife was over visiting us, "This is good for the two of you, because you aren't in each other's worlds." How true that is! Although we were pastors in the same town, we were from different worlds when talking about congregations or denominational issues. We all need such outlets. Our congregations' members come to church to talk to others about their jobs and lives. Where do we clergy go? Without outlets, colleagues to talk with, we can become isolated in our call.

My friend's connection through her brother did prove to be a good one. He brought me into his group of friends—a mixture of people from work and school, nearly all transplants to Michigan—and I learned a lot from them about how to find and make friends. Sometimes as clergy, we think our challenges are unique, and in some ways they are (Saturday nights are not the best time for us to go out). But in many ways, they are not. We have to do what everyone else does to meet and make friends. We have to engage in activities where there are other people around, and church activities don't count. I realize that this will be hardest for introverts, but trust me, it can be done, and it's worth it.

Has Boundaries, Is Not Bound

It is always hard to set and maintain personal boundaries. Today I am taking a day of study leave at a time when my head of staff is out of town. So naturally a congregation member died, and another one is in the hospital. This means that despite my attempts to garner some time for myself, I will be at the office. I hope that my lack of foresight will be an example for you. Taking time away when you might be "on call" is risky. If you need to leave town, or stay home and lock yourself in your house, or turn your phone off to have the time you need to take care of yourself, do that. Last Saturday night my phone rang. I did not hear it, and did not receive the message until 10:30 p.m. A member had called in desperation, because she was out of town and her friend's mother had died. I quickly decided that I do not need to be available all the time. The friend's mother, sad as her passing is for those who will miss her, is with God, and nothing I can do will change that. Moreover, no plans will be made between 7:00 p.m. Saturday and 2:00 p.m. Sunday. Yes, even funeral homes don't plan funerals with families on Saturday nights!

If you are like most young clergy, you probably have a cell phone and perhaps no landline. This means that it will be hard for you to separate your personal life from your professional life. Consider setting "cell hours" during which you will answer your phone. Screen your calls, particularly for "chatty Cathy" members, knowing that if a matter is important, the caller will leave a message. Use the same approach to deal with texting. You do not have to text a congregation member back immediately, especially during your personal time.

The mention of cell phones and texting leads us to social networking websites. These can be great for finding and making friends. No matter what you may think is possible with privacy settings, remember that your congregation members will find you on Facebook and other sites. (And don't think age matters. I have Facebook "friends" in their eighth decade of life.) Think before you post, and ask your friends to do the same, especially if you have had an account for a while and it has not previously included congregation members. On the other hand, if you have congregation members who want to know "what you do all day" on non-Sundays, Twitter and Facebook can be tools to show what you are up to, and that, yes, there is enough to do around the church for them to pay you full-time.

Setting these boundaries will be hard, and everyone will set them differently. Have a conversation with your church secretary about it. Consider the norms in your congregation. Think about what amount of communication from the church you would like when you are "off duty." You may adopt a call policy of "only in a dire emergency" or "never." You can tell the secretary that you want a phone call on your day off only if someone dies or is dying. If your position is primarily programmatic, then you may want calls on your day off if they pertain to volunteers dropping out of or signing up for an event. You may wish to have vacation days treated differently from days off.

Look at your situation and do what works for you and for your ministry. One of my friends told me the following story: "Last Saturday morning I got a phone message from a bride asking to get into the church. I am not doing the wedding, and she was instructed to make all her arrangements through an elder in the church. So, living in the manse next to the church, I did not return the call, cut off all the lights, and went upstairs. Does that make me a bad pastor?" The answer is "No!" Set boundaries and maintain them!

For those of us who have trouble saying no or setting those boundaries, sometimes it is easier if we have an excuse. For example, one clergyperson I know has declared Saturday "family day," so whenever there is a church event on Saturday, she reminds the church that it is family day and that if she is expected to be at the event, she will need child care. Having her kids there is a visible reminder that she is more than just the church's pastor. Others of us can use our husbands or other relationships as a reason we are not available for meetings and other events 24/7. One of my mentors declared Thursday evening "date night," and everyone in the two-thousand-plus-member congregation knew that he would therefore not be available on Thursday nights. Let's be honest—who is going to tell the pastor that he can't have a "date night"?

Some pastors find that owning a dog helps them set boundaries. The idea here is that a dog is high-maintenance enough that you may have to go home on your lunch break to let the dog out, and dogs require exercise, so you may be forced to become more active. As someone who recently took the dive into dog ownership, I can confirm that the new addition to my family has provided the excuse to run home right away after a day of meetings, and given my dog's antics, I am sure he will eventually supply me with a sermon illustration. Pets also give us something to think about besides ourselves and our work. Even though a bird won't need to be "let out" to go to the bathroom, it does require regular food and water, and unlike a houseplant, it can't really be ignored. Pets can provide hours of entertainment and comfort at the end of a long, hard day.

God Rested, and So Should You!

As a clergyperson, you have probably been given four weeks (with four Sundays) of vacation, which is what our counterparts in industry work an entire career to enjoy. Vacation is one of the few benefits with which we are "ahead" of our professional peers, but there is also a reason for this: we are potentially always on call. This past summer I returned from a five-day youth trip late Friday night, having driven for twelve hours. I returned to find that one member was hospitalized in critical condition, and that the organist had just been released from the hospital after a near-fatal bee sting. I was trying to enjoy one day of peace before preaching and leading worship Sunday morning when at 11:00 a.m. the phone rang. It was a member of the congregation whose brother had just died. So my day of peace included meeting him and his wife at the church for prayer. This is just what pastors do. Convenient or not, our job is to be with people when they are in need, showing them that God cares for them in their distress. (For the record, as tired as I was, I would not have chosen to be anywhere other than with that member and his wife that day.)

Our calling is a challenging one (often more so than industry), and it is for that reason that we have available on day one of a call all our vacation time for the year (as opposed to having to earn it month by month). Please do not let a calendar year go by without taking your full vacation. If you have trouble "finding the time," remind yourself that you are in this calling for the long haul, as in forty years! If you do not take your vacation time now and as you go, you may wind up being one of the many clergy nearing retirement who are just plain worn out. Do not become one of these people. It's unhealthy for you, and it will be unhealthy for the church. I am now working with a pastoral nominating committee, and one of the top requests the congregation has for its next pastor is that he or she "will be an example to us." Your church wants to look up to you, and they need you to be an example. I am not saying that you should be Wonder Woman, but you need to try to be the best authentic example you can be. Being authentic includes self-care. If you set an example for the congregation of being a Christian that does not include rest and care for yourself, you are giving members an unrealistic ideal that they will not be able to attain. You will leave the congregation constantly falling short and without grace. Show grace by modeling self-care. Give grace to yourself and others freely, just as Christ has done for you.

Also remember that you are setting a precedent for clergy who will follow you. If you set unrealistic standards for your position, you may burn out or leave another clergyperson with unrealistically big shoes to fill. A longtime former pastor in the church I serve refused to take a raise for more than twenty years. While I am sure he was a wonderful, humble example as a follower of Christ, his martyrdom left the church in a tough spot when it was time to hire his replacement. Overworking is no different from refusing a raise. Do not set unrealistic expectations for your congregation. I know you're a rock star, but just make sure you are keeping your boundaries, for you and for your parishioners. Besides, God took the seventh day off. What makes you think you're better than God?

Fit for Ministry

One of the books I read for a class during seminary was titled *Fit to Be a Pastor: A Call to Physical, Mental, and Spiritual Fitness.*

The book came complete with exercise diagrams in the back. I remember laughing with my classmates as we flipped through the images of a man doing toe-touches and other stretching activities. Maybe regularly working out is your thing; maybe it's not. The truth is that engaging in some kind of physical activity is good for you. Whether you take a leisurely walk around the block or join a yoga or a spin class, getting moving is a great way to reduce stress and work out all those frustrations that come with life. It can be a challenge to make working out a high priority. For this reason I recommend scheduling the time. If you can't haul yourself out of bed the morning after a late-night meeting to work out on your own, find a buddy. Need a different level of commitment? Sign up for a class. Once you've plunked down the money, it's hard to sleep through it or schedule a meeting that conflicts with it—which brings us to another point. Making self-care of your body a higher priority than day-to-day church work helps set boundaries.

Another way of committing to an exercise regimen is to set a goal for yourself. As terrifying as this may sound to you, several clergy colleagues and I have trained for and run a marathon (or more than one) while serving churches. Knowing you have to log a certain number of miles and hours outside the office, running (because it is hard to type a sermon on the treadmill) forces you to make exercise a high priority and can prevent you from putting off writing your sermon until your day off. The added benefit I have found from training for a race is the opportunity to set goals. As someone who went straight from high school to college and from college to seminary, I realized after a few years out of school that I really missed working toward a milestone. Training for a marathon gave me that goal, and it's a great conversation point when meeting people, as well as fuel for sermon illustrations on Philippians 3.

Maybe the marathon is too big of a goal for you. One thing I learned, once I dived into the world of running as an adult, is that nearly every race has a walk component. So if you simply want to train to walk a 5K, you can do that. If you have a medical condition that prevents you from running for an extended time, you may choose to walk and run at intervals for the race. There are many options and ways to work toward a goal that involves being physically active.

Take advantage of your surroundings. Cross-country skiing is big in Michigan, as is waterskiing. I have a colleague in Florida who learned to surf because of her proximity to the beach. There is something for everyone, but the onus is on you to take care of yourself in this way. No one in the congregation is going to ask you if you got your "workouts in" this week.

Taking Care of You

In seminary we talked about whether or not you should see a doctor who is a member of your congregation. I remember firmly deciding that I was unwilling to have a congregation member see me naked. Upon moving to my first call, I did what I suspect a lot of us who are pretty healthy do: I put off making a doctor's appointment. Finally, after eight months or so, I made an appointment with a doctor in a neighboring city who was sure not to be a member of the congregation. When I went in for my first appointment, I realized that this office employed medical students from the university near my congregation. As I was walking toward the exam room, much to my horror I saw one of the med students who attended my church! Once in the room with the nurse, I explained that I was a pastor, that the student attended my church, and that I was uncomfortable with her being present in the room. Fortunately the nurse understood, although I don't know what she told the student. All I know is that I was unwilling to discuss my sexual history or how much I drink or smoke with someone who listens to me preach.

While it may be inconvenient to leave town for all my medical and dental appointments, I think it is worth it. If you, like me, did a clinical pastoral education (CPE) residency, then you know that everyone in the office has access to the medical charts. The lab tech or nurse who is a congregation member will therefore know what medications you are taking. I don't know about you, but that is information I don't want shared unless I choose to share it.

Caring for our health is not just focusing on our physical health but also tending to our mental and emotional health. Being in ministry can be hard, and trying to balance ministry with spousal and family obligations can be even harder. Many denominations have special funds for clergy who wish to seek counseling, beyond what health insurance provides. As someone who has availed herself of counseling in the past, I cannot recommend it enough. Think of it this way. You spend all week listening to other people's problems. For just one hour a week, someone will listen to you, and that person and space are safe. You know what you need to do to take care of yourself. Don't end up sick or in need of help without anyone to turn to. Set up those doctor relationships soon after arriving in your new call.

Taking Care of Your Spirit

As I was preparing for ordination, I was told by a member of a committee overseeing my process that I needed to walk for twenty minutes each day as a spiritual and physical discipline. I told a seminary classmate about this, and he was shocked at how presumptuous this man was. Why would his spiritual discipline work for me? Different things work for different people, and different practices work best at different points in our lives.

As spiritual leaders, we constantly give to others, and we can find ourselves growing dry. We fight this tendency by taking the time we need for refreshment, which can come in many forms—perhaps daily devotional reading (or listening), time spent in prayer daily, or work with a spiritual director. Perhaps your spirituality is more physical, such as walks in the woods or yoga. Perhaps it is regular meditation or spending quiet time on the porch with a cup of tea. However we find it, we all need time to hear God's still small voice.

Keep on Learning

If you were like me, you left seminary so full of knowledge (almost dangerously so) that you thought you would never run dry. The truth is that you will eventually run out of ideas—or figure out which classes you should have taken, or realize that your material is outdated. Continuing education is time and money given to us both to keep our skills sharp and to give us time to rejuvenate. There will be periods of time in ministry when you will feel so overworked and behind that although you can't fathom finding the time to work ahead, you can't stand the idea of continually running from week to week as you have been. Let me assure you, it is okay to take study leave or continuing-education time to work on worship plans, prepare sermons for special days, or write curriculum. If you do not have time to do this—along with visiting members, attending meetings, and supervising the work crew fixing the building—then take time designated for study leave (or continuing education) to prepare for sermons or write curriculum. It is okay; that is part of what that time is for.

Continuing education or study leave is also provided to allow you to keep your skills sharp. One of the best ways to do this is to have a mentor (or perhaps several, because let's face it, no one but Jesus is perfect). Having a mentor, whether nearby or far away, can help us stay sane on those tough days and provide us with the sounding board or advice we need when we are in a pinch. Some denominational structures provide mentors, and if you are working on a staff, your supervisor may be a sort of built-in mentor. Open your eyes and look around, and begin early to identify your mentors.

Then there are conferences. If you can imagine something you would like to know, there is probably a conference where you can learn it. Besides that, conferences are great ways to connect with friends, to network, and to get away from the daily grind of ministry, allowing you to get perspective on the work you are doing. They can provide time for discernment and rejuvenation and have the added bonus of being something that laypeople are likely to be familiar with and consider beneficial.

What Is a Day Off for, Besides Laundry?

I remember sitting in a booth at a restaurant. A group of us clergy were out to dinner at a conference when one of my newly ordained colleagues leaned across the table and said, "What do you do on your days off? Besides laundry?" This is a big question for those of us in ministry. What do we do with that one-seventh of our time when we aren't expected to be in the office? Do we go into the office in jeans? Do we stay home and do laundry, clean house, and take care of all that stuff that didn't get done the other six days of the week? I have to admit that I had always dreamed of more for my days off. I had always dreamed that they would be used for yoga class and volunteering, when in reality, I typically pad around the house in my PJs until noon, then eat a leisurely breakfast and, on a good day, start the laundry. I think there is one thing days off should not be used for, and that is work, although I have on more than one occasion broken that rule. So days off are and will always be a struggle for me.

I once worked with a Catholic priest who referred to his day off as his "beauty day." Trust me, he did spend the day on errands and personal grooming. (He had the nicest cuticles I have ever seen.) If a Catholic priest can do it, so can we. Let's dream a little, spell out some things we would do on our day off if we could do whatever we wanted. I'd sleep in, read a good

book, go for a run, go shopping, have lunch with a friend, be
alone all day, and not talk to anyone I didn't want to talk to,
learn to bake the perfect pie, take tae kwon do lessons, take a
nap, go on a long bike ride, watch lots of movies, go out dancing, learn to play the piano, get a massage, paint my nails, spend
the day wandering around a museum, talk all day on the phone
with a good friend, start that craft project I've been thinking
about, spend time with family, spend time with my cat. Now
it's your turn.

Back to reality. Of course, there will always be laundry and
errands to run. If you want your day off to be more than life-
maintenance, however, then make it more than that. Make a
priority of those things you want to do. More often than not,
the things you do in your free time will end up feeding your
ministry. Think of how many sermon illustrations you've run
across during off-work hours. Using your day off for more than
chores and leftover work from the week is important in maintaining yourself in ministry.

Jesus Already Saved Everyone

As a youth I read a book by Christian education professor Rodger
Nishioka, in which he said he had a sign in his office announcing, "The savior has come, and you are not it." As a teen I posted
the phrase in my bedroom, and I have carried this reminder
with me. If you, like me, are prone to seeking perfection, this is a
good message for you. You are a kind, loving, and caring person.
You're probably in ministry because you want to help people.
That is great; don't lose that. However, if you are feeding your
self-esteem or need to be needed from ministering, you have to
find another outlet. There are plenty of volunteer organizations
that would love your expertise. You may enjoy the idea of rush-
ing off to the hospital in an emergency, but you cannot live your
life in a constant state of turmoil. It is not good for you, and
it is not good for the church. Practice letting go. You will be

surprised at how much the congregation can do without you. Besides, isn't part of our role helping Christians own *their* ministry? How are they going to be disciples of Christ if all they do is watch you disciple?

The Girlfriends' Checklist

- Make nearby friends. You can't do this ministry or life thing alone. You have to make friends, and the ones in worship on Sunday morning won't be enough. Find at least one person within a half-day's drive whom you can count as a friend.
- Use your day off and take vacation. God rested on the seventh day. Shouldn't you follow the divine example?
- Care for your physical self. Go to the doctor, and get active!
- Remember your spiritual life. Part of this God-gig means having time with God. Don't neglect *your* own prayer time.
- Keep learning. What you learned in seminary won't be enough for forty years of ministry. Sign up for that conference.
- Realize that you are not Superwoman and be okay with it! Jesus is perfect; you're not; get over it.

·9·

Tiresome, Taxing, and Toxic

DIFFICULT SITUATIONS IN MINISTRY

Amanda Adams Riley and Amy Morgan

••••

M aybe you've heard the common expression, "The church is a hospital for sinners, not a hotel for saints." If you got into ministry thinking that the church is a utopia inhabited by "good Christian people" and free of inappropriate sexual relationships, addictions, and embezzlement, we hate to be the ones to tell you, but it's not. As good Presbyterians, we are always cognizant of Calvin's notion that we are "mired in sin." If we take sin seriously, we know that the church cannot be free of sin, and we won't be surprised to see the dysfunction—unhealthy behaviors, broken relationships, and systemic disorder—caused by sin in our own ministry settings.

When we are looking for a call, we do all we can to ask the right questions while recognizing that no situation is perfect. But sometimes no matter how hard we try, we end up in bad situations in ministry. This is unfortunately even more common in a first call and often more common for women, perhaps because we are eager to find a place to serve and will therefore "settle." When we realize that our dream congregation doesn't think we are the right fit, we may have to accept a position with some—well, challenges. Difficult situations can arise among other staff members in multistaff churches, between church leaders or strong personalities, within personal relationships or situations, or in relation to just about any major event or stressor in the life of a church.

We categorize these difficult ministry situations as *tiresome*, *taxing*, and *toxic*, and you will want to approach each category differently.

Tiresome situations are challenging but also have a transitory property (a sanctuary renovation or a transition in staffing, for example). You might simply live with some tiresome situations because part of being in community is coping with personalities that you find challenging (a staff member with different work habits or a confrontational church member, for instance).

Taxing situations are ongoing and wear you down (a church member who wants to micromanage your schedule, or one who doesn't trust your expertise and is continuously undermining your work). Taxing situations are different from tiresome situations because they cannot be tolerated. Ignoring a taxing situation can lead to burnout and even cause you to leave a church.

Toxic situations involve deep-seated and long-lasting issues with the way the congregation or the staff functions as a whole. Toxic situations also may involve a traumatic event in the congregation, such as highly inappropriate or criminal activity by a leader, or a tragedy affecting the congregation or leadership. Toxic situations are exceptionally difficult to address and may be transformed only with intentional work on the part of the leaders. Again, these situations cannot be ignored or tolerated, as they will be detrimental to your ministry and will affect your personal life.

As a leader in a challenging situation, you need to be able to recognize that you are working in unusually difficult circumstances. Sometimes you might become so enmeshed in your ministry that the dysfunction feels normal. This quandary can cause you to shoulder the blame or to question your fitness for ministry. At times, you may sense that something is wrong in your ministry environment, but sometimes it is difficult to identify *what* is wrong, how bad the problem is, and what course of action will be most appropriate and effective. Give yourself time and space to decipher whether you are dealing with a situation that is tiresome, taxing, or toxic before you make judgments about your ministry and how to handle the situation.

Tiresome Situations

No one, I hope, ever told you that ministry would be easy. But, as the Sheryl Crow song goes, "No one ever said it would be this hard."[1] Ministry can wear you out, girlfriend! Realize that you will, over time, adjust to the pace. In Amy's first year of ministry, she had to come home and take a nap between morning worship and afternoon youth activities. Being an introvert, she found four hours of smiles, handshakes, teaching, public speaking, and informal conversation tiresome. Obviously, such activities are part of the job description of any minister. But she was shocked by how exhausting it was in the beginning. Four years later, Amy can stay up all night at a youth lock-in on Friday, attend a church potluck on Saturday night, and go all day Sunday without a nap. It's not always pretty, but she can do it. You will also build stamina for those aspects of ministry that tire you out.

Some situations we would classify as tiresome because they involve transition. Any time the church building undergoes renovation, changes are made in staffing, or a congregation undertakes a new ministry, anxiety levels rise. Much of this anxiety will be focused on you as a leader in the church. Obviously, there is a difference between a building project and a staff transition, but the behavior and unease of members will look similar. As annoying and tiresome as these transitional periods can be, they are simply that: transitional. The job of the pastor is to be a listening ear and to provide support for the congregation during the transition.

A colleague of Amanda's used to say, "Church would be great if it weren't for the people!" Even though church wouldn't be church without people, living in community is difficult, and relationships with congregation members or staff are sometimes tiresome. However, it's important to realize that our calling is to be in community with people despite our differences. Sometimes those things that drive you crazy about a person can be her greatest assets. If you are a slightly disorganized person, you might feel insecure around your perfectly organized Christian education director. When she takes notes at meetings and later e-mails them to everyone, you might think she's showing off a bit. When she follows up with you to see if you've gotten around to completing a project you had discussed, you might think she is being invasive or even controlling. However, if you are able to view her organizational prowess as a strength rather than an annoyance, you can be grateful that she helps you remember what went on in those endless meetings and keeps you on task when your to-do list (if you can even find it) gets out of hand. Likewise, if you are "type A" and like to plan and work ahead, but your fellow staff members prefer to work at the last minute, strive to see the flexibility that waiting can make possible in a situation. Everyone has gifts, and learning to see others' strengths and how they may complement your own will help you get along in the body of Christ.

Sometimes we have to look beyond the obvious when dealing with tiresome situations. Perhaps the head of the mission committee is a total control freak, rarely delegates, and when he does, checks up on your work obsessively. He has begun to ruin your life by calling and e-mailing constantly about totally inconsequential matters and even—*gasp!*—dropping by your office unexpectedly to suck up huge chunks of your day. This relationship can feel taxing. But then consider that his job is in jeopardy, his marriage is on the rocks, and his youngest daughter just left for college. His life is totally out of control, and this mission committee is the only thing going well in his life. He may be dropping by your office for pastoral support as much as for mission matters. Now, you can't take ten hours a week to manage this one congregation member, but you can compassionately deal with him, set appropriate boundaries, and help him find ways to feel more in control without controlling your life.

Every church has its "energy vampires." The question is, are they allowed to run rampant, infecting the entire congregation? Every church has staff members and congregation members you won't be best friends with. The question is, does the church have people and protocols in place that help you navigate your working relationships and mediate your differences? Every church has power struggles. The question is, will these struggles leave you feeling worthless and helpless, or are there enough healthy leaders in the church to get everyone playing for the same team? These questions determine the difference between situations that are tiresome and those that are taxing.

TAKING CHARGE OF THE TIRESOME

If your tiresome situation is transitional, taking charge is part waiting game and part focusing on the things you can control—namely, your own responses to the situation. When the same church member tells you for the fifth time this month that the construction crew is blocking her preferred parking spot, and you remind her for the fifth time that everyone is experiencing inconveniences during the building project, you may need to take a few deep breaths and pray before she speaks to you again next week.

When the tiresome situation has to do with an individual, you have two choices. You can either have a conversation with him in which you make clear any specific requests about your working relationship, or you can adapt your style and behavior to his. No one wins and little gets done when one person is always overwhelming the others with details and working far ahead. Likewise, if one person is always waiting until the last minute, her behavior can be crazy-making for everyone else on the team. However you choose to go forward, whether seeking a change in someone else's behavior or adapting your own, working with differing personality types is part of living in community, and life in general. Sometimes living in Christian community is about compromise and getting along, more than about being "right" or getting "my way."

As you wait out or work through tiresome situations, self-care is extremely important. When you aren't getting your needs met, it is always harder to deal with circumstances or personalities that wear you out. Take time to focus on the things that drew you to ministry. Affirm your gifts and skills by rereading notes with the kind things people have written to you or remembering positive things people have said about you. (One of Amanda's mentors taught her to keep all the kind notes that had ever been written to her by church members so that she could read them on days when she was feeling down.) And finally, try not to get caught up in drama (or create more drama) that prevents you from being an excellent pastor.

Taxing Situations

As with tiresome situations, taxing situations come in two forms. One form concerns the culture of the church, and the other is focused on relationships with specific individuals. Both situations require thoughtful action if you are to effect a transition into healthy ministry.

The first year in ministry is exciting. You are looking forward to Advent, Lent, Holy Week, Easter, and the long stretch of ordinary time. Planning and envisioning each season's worship, music, education, mission, and other programs can be fulfilling. Once you've spun the liturgical wheel a few times, however, the ins and outs of the program year can feel less like a spiritual journey through the life of Christ and the early church and more like a hamster wheel with no exit. Some of our colleagues who have been around the liturgical block a few more times than we have say that January and July used to be "quiet" months in the church. Now the church, like the rest of the world, is on a 24/7/365 schedule, and the effect on the church and its leaders is taxing. We feel the need to run programs and have church events that meet everyone's needs all the time.

As busy as the church can be, there will always be important and necessary things to be done, and they may not always seem to be what you spent years in school preparing for. There is a lot of grunt work involved in ministry. We can get worn out by those aspects of our ministry that are less than romantic, or we can find ways to understand them as part of our call. On the other hand, your ministry may reach a point at which you are being taxed by tasks that have no relationship to healthy and effective ministry in the church and, in fact, might hamper good ministry. That point comes when you look up from the daily grind of ministry and realize that you aren't doing what you love anymore, or that what you are doing no longer comes from a place of feeling called, but from one of feeling obligated. This can happen when we take on too much in the name of being "helpful" and replace the tasks of clergy with tasks that can be done by laypeople.

Churches are good at starting new programs and not great at ending existing programs. Every church needs to ask at some point, "Are we doing too much?" Are our programs effective in meeting the mission of our church? Are we doing this Advent tree decorating/lighting/chrismon/children's service out of habit or conviction? If you find yourself feeling as though your job is to run from one religious program to the next, making each one bigger and better, without any real thought about why the program *needs to be better* or to whom goes the glory for this event, perhaps it is time to stop and discern—to discern where God is calling the church or a specific ministry and how that ministry helps further God's work in this world. Many churches we know take breaks from programming and business meetings during seasons like Lent or Advent or with a change in staff. It is important to take time to hear God's call to you and your ministry. It is nearly impossible to hear God when you are racing from the church's tutoring program to an evening dinner meeting followed by a Lenten planning meeting. There is nothing wrong with stopping programs to evaluate, discern, pray, and do the work of visioning.

As clergy, we are called and expected to preach and teach, both of which require time for study and prayer. We are also expected to visit the sick and shut-in, offering support, guidance, and prayer. Our well-intentioned desire both to keep programs alive and to do the unique work of clergy leads to overfunctioning. Moreover, when volunteers back out or staff cuts happen, the implicit assumption is that those of us who are paid will pick up the slack. The problem here is that, at some point, we go too far and end up carrying the entire program, or worse, the bulk of all the programs. We end up in these situations with the best of intentions. You don't want that mission with the local soup kitchen to die off, even though you are scrambling each month to beg three more people to go with you to cook and serve dinner. You know that the mid-week Lenten service is meaningful to the five people who were showing up, but the ten hours it takes you and the church musician each week to prepare for the service in the middle of an already busy season seems excessive. It is just hard to let go when we believe that the effort matters to someone or even could matter again one day. When you find yourself picking up lots of loose ends, keep in mind that any work you do that could be done by a volunteer takes away the opportunity for another Christian to serve. Hold back from picking up every ball that gets dropped, so that another disciple has space to come alongside and join the work of the kingdom.

Taxing Traits

While ministry itself can be taxing, the people we must deal with can sometimes challenge us. Once when Amanda was conducting an informational interview, she was told by a pastor about his experience as an associate. He said that whenever his head of staff told him to "jump," he was more or less expected to ask "how high?" on the way up. It was clear from the conversation that he would expect any associate he worked with to respond as he had been required to. (At the time, his church was searching for an associate pastor. The previous one had lasted only two years, and that had been a decade earlier.) This exchange raised some red flags for Amanda. Years earlier, she had held one position (thankfully, it was not in a church) that was so difficult she dreaded going into the office. The head of the nonprofit she worked for was a micromanager. Part of her position included prepping crafts for children at a weekly meeting, so this meant that from time to time, she and other staff members would be sitting at their desks cutting out shapes from construction paper. It was not uncommon for their boss to walk by, and then stop and glare, as if to say, "So, you're playing with colored paper on my time." She would even walk up behind Amanda, lean over her desk, stare at her computer monitor, and ask what she was doing. Having worked for a micromanager, Amanda knew the telltale signs, and she knew that it was not a personality type she worked well with. Once she realized that the pastor she was interviewing was a micromanager, she knew they would not work well together and that she should not entertain the position available at the church he served. Some people deal well with micromanagers. Others do not. And in the church, micromanagers come in all forms. It could be your direct supervisor, an overeager volunteer, or a board member who sees all of your time as "church time." But for most people, working with micromanagers is taxing, and over time, it can wear you down.

Another taxing kind of relationship involves working with flawed individuals. Whether they are congregation members (whom you may be able to shepherd), other staff members, or your supervisor, these relationships can be draining. With flawed congregation members, you may find yourself constantly picking up what they drop at the last minute. In some cases you may be able to work with them and help them improve, but if they are simply unreliable because their personal lives are in disorder or even chaos, or because church activities are not a priority, then you will be best served by recognizing this and accepting that this is just how they are. Although challenging personalities can impede your ministry, the reality is that in the church, unlike the business world, you cannot "fire" volunteers. You can, however, steer them toward areas of involvement that are not quite as time-sensitive as, say, running the sound system for Sunday worship. If this person is in a key area of the church, some creative restructuring of the ministry area they are involved in may help you manage the effects of their personality.

If you work in a multistaff environment, you probably work collaboratively on some tasks or projects. Flawed staff members, particularly supervisors, can be frustrating to work with because you may find yourself defending their poor work habits or cleaning up after them. Finding yourself in this situation over and over again can lead to burnout. You should not have regular anxiety dreams about what your head of staff has or has not done. Dealing with this predicament can be complicated. You may begin minimizing the amount of work you do together to preserve your own sanity. If his lack of ability continues to be an ongoing issue that affects not just your own ability to engage in good life-giving ministry, but also the ability of the church to function without major intervention from you, it may be time for you to seek another church.

Supervisors who fear conflict can also be challenging to work with. On the one hand, they can be great to work with, because you know they will never yell at you. On the other hand, they can be miserable to deal with, because you know they will never defend you when a congregation member is upset about something you have done. Conflict-avoidant supervisors or even congregational leaders can be annoying to work with or downright dangerous, depending on the severity of the problems. If the supervisor is constantly placating the curmudgeon in the congregation, that is one thing. It's not usually worth the effort to go toe-to-toe with the eighty-something-year-old who tells the staff every week that the communion serving pieces weren't set out correctly. But if a supervisor is unable to settle real disagreements between staff members or between staff and congregational members, that is another thing. If a supervisor isn't comfortable defending a staff person against the complaints of a member or vice versa, the work environment for staff can quickly become untenable. You do not want a supervisor who will not support you during difficult disagreements. In trying times, a supervisor who avoids conflict can be taxing and, if the situation is left unaddressed, it can wear you down.

Making Transitions in the Taxing Situation

When your day-to-day work is wearing you down, take a look at your to-do list, or where your time is spent. A year into Amanda's first associate pastor position, she was feeling like a "program monkey." All she did all day, every day, was organize programs, and while this played to her strengths as a hyper-organized "type A" person, it did not fulfill her call to ministry.

After some time in prayer and discernment, she realized that she needed to do more pastoral care and to spend more time in worship preparation to feel that she was using her gifts fully and not simply outlining retreat schedules and recruiting volunteers. Sometimes the day-to-day work of ministry can feel less like a calling that requires ordination and more like "just a job," one in which we fail to see the fruits of countless hours spent recruiting volunteers. After a conversation with her head of staff, Amanda was able to spend more of her time visiting members and less time organizing programs.

If the daily grind of the church's program year is what you find taxing, then it may be time for a conversation with the church leadership about programming mindfully and not simply developing or continuing programs for the sake of programs. Intentional programming has a clear, ministry-based purpose. It is not programming that comes about because "we've always had children's Sunday school." From time to time it is important to take a step back, evaluate the church's ministry and programs, and make sure they are being carried out with a purpose and goal in mind and not simply as something to do. There is plenty of biblical witness to support taking a year of Jubilee to let the ground lie fallow, so that it can once again yield a bountiful harvest.

If the taxing part of your life comes from working with a micromanager, flawed church leader, or a conflict-avoiding boss, any change in the situation will likely have to be initiated by you. It will always be easier to change your own behavior than to change the behavior of someone else. Sometimes the best thing you can do is simply to accept that you work with someone who is difficult. Once you accept that individual's personality and mode of operating, you can better discern how to work with and, if need be, around him or her. Sometimes, however, taxing behaviors can be so extreme that what might have been a taxing situation becomes toxic.

Toxic Situations

The signs of a toxic situation can be obvious. You may have nightmares or even physical symptoms. When serving one congregation, Amanda had chest pains during staff meetings (not a good thing for a twenty-something). For a time during part of her first year in ministry, Amy had a panic attack every time she turned the car in the direction of the church. That's when she knew her situation was toxic.

It is possible to become so comfortable in a toxic environment that we don't even realize the situation is getting worse. Despite signs that situations are toxic, sometimes it takes fresh eyes to help you see what is going on. If you relay a church story to a friend and she is shocked by what happened, you may want to step back and analyze your environment. We have many friends who have been in situations that slowly became toxic. Make sure you have a sounding board so that you can recognize the toxicity in your situation. Other signs of toxicity include high staff turnover, a major membership rift or exodus, or unusual secrecy in the church.

The least subtle toxic situation is one in which misconduct is involved. Unfortunately, misconduct is often hidden, so you may recognize strange behavior before the root of the issue comes to light. In the church, misconduct usually involves one of three issues: (1) sex (for example, viewing pornography in the office, engaging in extramarital sex), (2) money (for example, embezzlement), or (3) addictions, whether to drugs, alcohol, or something else (sometimes sexual misconduct and addiction overlap). Here's the tricky part with misconduct: the church has a tendency to believe the best about its own and to look the other way for as long as possible, ignoring the truth until ignorance is no longer bliss (or even a possibility). We have seen churches side with an alcoholic pastor over all reason, so even when misconduct comes to light, be prepared for the toxicity to continue. If you are unfortunate enough to discover the misconduct and the church sides with the perpetrator (which happens more often than anyone would like to admit), you may have to leave. Even though you are not at fault and you did not cause the problem, the dysfunctional system may eject you so that it can survive.

Many toxic situations are more subtle than those involving misconduct. Often they involve personality clashes or struggles for control. One friend was in a situation where major power plays and personality conflicts beleaguered the church staff. Finally, the associate pastor was called in by the personnel committee, whose members intended to take him to task for something another staff member had complained about. When the committee members heard the associate's side of the story, they realized that there was a seriously toxic situation among the church staff.

A truly toxic situation is one in which the environment will continue to be dysfunctional even when those involved in the conflict leave. We have all seen churches with a history of sexual misconduct repeat similar patterns years later, or churches with chronic infighting among staff repeat the behavior years later with completely different staff members. In recognizing a toxic situation in her church, Amy's head of staff looked back at a speech about the state of the church delivered to the church board ten years (and three pastors) earlier and discovered that the same speech could have been given to the board today. These types of situations have deep-seated origins and require thoughtful and often professional intervention.

TONIC FOR THE TOXIC SITUATION

Savvy churches have tools in place—operations manuals, personnel protocols, insurance, and sexual-misconduct policies—to guard against and deal with toxic situations. Human resources professionals from the secular world have helped some churches get up to date with some of the essentials. The church is not the secular business world, however. It's not the world of professional counseling or education. The church has borrowed techniques and best practices from all of these fields, but it is a unique social organism. Unlike other nonprofits, community organizations, or for-profit organizations, religious communities are bound together by something other than finances, ideals, interests, or social norms. The church is the body of Christ, a community of Christ-followers and sanctuary for saints and sinners alike.

The cure for a toxic environment is more than regulations. Leaders and members alike need to shift the culture, to change their behavior. Institutional change of this magnitude requires skills and training that you may not possess early in your ministry. This is when you need to reach out for help. In the case of the friend we mentioned earlier, the personnel committee, at the associate pastor's suggestion, brought in a consultant who listened to the staff members individually, helped them work out their group dynamics, and provided leadership training for the head of staff. Within a few months, the associate pastor experienced a complete turnaround in his ministry environment. The associate had to have the strength to stand up for himself in this situation and the wisdom to seek outside help for the church. He hadn't worked with ministry consultants before, but he researched several options for the personnel committee to choose from.

This kind of help can do more than heal one set of broken relationships. Outside consultants should also equip church leaders, staff and laypeople alike, so they can work together to address systemic issues they observe in the church. The assistance these consultations can provide will likely outlast your individual ministry in that congregation. As an alternative to professional consultants (who can be pricey), you may have ministry mentors who can help you navigate a toxic situation. In some denominations, judicatory staff can intervene in toxic situations and facilitate healing and education.

Toxic situations are often associated with high staff turnover, either because the church blames the leadership for the toxicity and asks a leader to leave, or because the staff flees from the toxic environment. While a change in staffing is not always the answer, sometimes toxic situations can be addressed through new leadership. Amy's church seemed to have a revolving door in the head-of-staff position for about twenty-five years before she came to serve there as an associate. Amy arrived just as yet another head of staff was leaving—after serving there less than five years. There certainly seemed to be some systemic issues in the church, but Amy couldn't rightly identify what they were or how to address them. After two years of turmoil, a new head of staff arrived. Because he had extensive training in Bowen Family Systems theory and had worked with a number of troubled congregations through the church's judicatory bodies, he was able quickly and effectively to begin to address the problems that had plagued the church for years.[2] With stable leadership, finances, and facilities, the church went from anxious and grumbling to positive and hopeful in a short time.

Sometimes It's Not Just about the Church

In ministry, the lines between personal and professional relationships are often blurred. While there was plenty of toxicity in Amy's church during her first two years of ministry, there were also a number of stressors in her personal life as she juggled raising a young child with the demands of ministry, lived with financial stress while her husband looked for a steady job, and struggled to create a stable support network. While you don't want to blame yourself for a toxic working environment, you also don't want to blame the church for your personal struggles. As you navigate what might seem to be a toxic situation, be sure to draw clear lines between your personal and professional struggles, so you can clearly discern how to proceed in both areas of your life. A spiritual director or personal counselor can be extremely helpful—in addition, of course, to your girlfriends.

Whatever your challenging situation, and however you choose to move forward, know that you are not the first pastor to wrestle with difficult situations in ministry, and you will not be the last. Seek out people you trust who will walk with you through the tough times so that you can emerge wiser and with a commitment to love and serve God's people.

The Girlfriends' Checklist

- Discern what kind of situation you are in—tiresome, taxing, or toxic.
- Get someone trustworthy to be your sounding board as you figure out how to deal with your situation.
- Make sure to engage in good self-care as you wait out or navigate tiresome situations or relationships.
- Get off the hamster wheel occasionally to evaluate your program load. If your tasks have become taxing, consider delegating or cutting back.
- Learn how to work with, or around, those personalities that are taxing to your ministry.
- Ask yourself if outside expertise is needed in toxic situations, and be prepared to seek out help from consultants, mentors, or higher governing bodies.
- Look at the role your personal life may play in the difficult situation you are experiencing.

·10·

When the Grass Looks Greener

TRANSITIONS IN MINISTRY

Melissa Lynn DeRosia and Amy Morgan

• • • •

Maybe your tonic isn't working, and you feel trapped in a toxic environment. Maybe your ministry has lost passion and drive, or you feel ineffectual in your current call. Maybe your life circumstances have changed, and your call is no longer a good match. Or maybe you just feel that it's time for a change. If you have prayed and discussed and discerned, if you have done all that is in your power to fulfill your call to ministry in this church, and you are starting to feel as though God is calling you to shepherd another flock or to pursue a different vocation— read this chapter.

Greener Grass

Discerning whether it is time to leave a call requires asking yourself why you are feeling called to leave the place where you are serving, where you will go next, and why. One challenge that many pastors face in the discernment process is failing to recognize that some aspects of serving the church, and the church itself, don't change. Whether you serve a small, rural congregation in the South or a large-membership church in the East, whether you're a Midwestern associate pastor or a West Coast solo pastor, the church will still be the church, no matter where you go and what you do.

And the church is made up of people. No matter what church you serve, you'll encounter dysfunctional families, back-stabbing gossips, hypercritical leaders, and every other kind of annoying personality you can think of. Whereas people might have to restrain their less-attractive personality traits to hold down a job during the week, those qualities are unleashed in the church community, because this is a place where they have relationships with people they trust and where they aren't afraid to be who God created them to be. You could see this authenticity as a beautiful thing and God's gift to us in the community of Christ-followers. Or people could just drive you crazy.

Before you begin dreaming that you would be perfectly happy and fulfilled if you could just get away from this person or that situation, if you could just be on the West Coast where people are more relaxed, or on the East Coast where people are more sophisticated, or in the South where people know not to hold Sunday school during worship, or in the North where people aren't so transient—wake up and smell the church coffee. Getting rid of one set of problems only makes room for a different set of problems. The question to ask yourself is not "Where would I be perfectly happy and fulfilled in ministry?" The question is "Do I want to tackle the set of problems I now face, or do I want to take on some completely unknown set of problems?" At some point in your ministry, the new set of problems will be the more enticing proposition.

God is the one who "makes me lie down in green pastures," but we have to first be able to say, "The LORD is my shepherd, I shall not want" (Ps. 23:1–2). We all enter ministry with at least a few fairy-tale notions of what it will be like: we will be respected as a "reverend"; we will feel close to God as we meaningfully serve God's people; we will transform lives with the good news of Jesus Christ. By the grace of God, all of these wonderful things do happen in your ministry. But we often don't have time or energy to notice how people look up to us, how God is with us and working through us, or how God is at work in the lives of those we serve—because we are too busy writing newsletters, crafting a stewardship campaign, getting quotes for the cost of a new roof, and putting out fires (sometimes literally).

Before you yearn for those greener pastures, make sure you have first taken time to let go of your wants and assess your needs. Make sure you've looked at what God is really doing with you in your current call. Talk with friends, mentors, or complete strangers who minister in other places, particularly places that look more appealing than where you are now. Find out how they feel about their pasture and their flock. Look at what options are realistically available to you. Some positions require a certain number of years of experience, so it may not be practical for you to move from the position you're in to the position you want right now.

Once you have gathered this information, you can better assess where the green pastures really are. In taking a closer look at your own ministry, you may find green shoots right under your feet.

Failure and Faithfulness

Despite all your best intentions to be faithful to your sense of call, maintaining boundaries, and putting a strong network of support in place, you will reach a time in your call when you don't feel so—well, called. Not all ministry calls end in frustration and disappointment. Transitions in ministry can be the result of various changes—in the church, in your life situation, and in your gifts and skills. Although churches change slowly, they do change. The wants and needs of the church to which you were called may evolve during your ministry, or you may help the members gain clarity about their ministry in the community. In such cases, the ministry the congregation feels called to may no longer fit with your own sense of call, or your gifts and skills. A woman who enters ministry without a spouse or child, and who later marries and starts a family, may find that the ministry she began as a single person no longer fits with the demands of family life. As you gain experience in ministry, you will grow and change. Through continuing education, mentoring, and on-the-job training, you'll develop new skills and discover new gifts. At some point, your gifts and skills may no longer be applicable in your current call. You may feel the need for a new ministry environment where you can be more effective and continue to grow.

Sensing a call to leave your church may feel like a failure on your part. Many of us in ministry are great at blaming ourselves when things go wrong. Thinking that you've failed your church in some way may lead to feelings of guilt. Believing that you've failed God in your calling may lead to a crisis of faith. First, remember that when we fail, we never fail alone. The church has the responsibility of supporting your ministry, and it may have failed you in some ways. Second, remember that the "the wind blows where it chooses, and you hear the sound of it, but you do not know where it comes from or where it goes. So it is with everyone who is born of the Spirit" (John 3:8). God empowers us in ministry, and you may truly be called in another direction.

Being called to another church or area of ministry does not always need to be understood as a failure, but it can be frustrating when you believe that God has called you to one place and now it seems that God is calling you to another. Considering the end of your calling to a particular church, or perhaps sensing a call to leave ministry entirely, can strain your relationship with God. The experience is often exasperating and depressing. We pour ourselves into our ministries, we make ourselves vulnerable, we put our lives in God's hands, and sometimes we don't get to see the fruits of our labors. As much as this outcome may feel like failure, it is truly part of the call to ministry. Just as death is part of life, so the end of our call is part of the call itself. The challenge is to remain faithful to the call through the conclusion and transition.

Most of us have asked at one time or another, "How will I know when I am no longer called to live out ministry in this location?" If you have been in ministry only two or three years, this question can be especially challenging. It can take a year or more to learn about a congregation and build relationships with the members of the church and the surrounding community. The possibility of ending those relationships and starting over again in a new church may seem an insurmountable task. We all enter into ministry hoping to engage in deep and lasting relationships with our congregations. We hope for stability in our lives and in the life of the church. But this is not always God's plan for us. God may use us to guide a church through a wilderness time, to help a congregation make the transition from one thing to another. Some people call this role "unintentional interim" ministry. The fact is, there is no ideal or predictable timeline for a call. We know pastors whose first call was their only call and lasted for decades. We know others who moved on after less than two years. The length of time you have served in a calling is not necessarily relevant when discerning whether it is time to move on. No matter how long you have served in your first call, if you are trying to discern where to go now or next, you are not alone. We all have moments when we'd rather be working a nine-to-five job and taking the family camping on the weekends. We all have moments when we feel that our ministry is stuck, that our sermons are dispassionate or even insincere, or that we just don't know how we can possibly work with *that* colleague or church member any longer. But we can get through those moments. The harder part is knowing that your longing for other pastures is no longer a moment, but a movement of the Spirit, a push from God to move in another direction. Girlfriend, this is one of the hardest times in ministry.

Transitions in Ministry

We hope that a call to a new ministry feels energizing and positive. Some of our girlfriends have felt a call to a different kind of ministry. Some have felt called to full-time parenting. Some have felt called to a new ministry context (urban, rural, smaller church, bigger church). And some have felt called to another vocation entirely. Whatever transition you are considering, the discernment process can be challenging, sometimes lengthy, and even heartbreaking. As you begin your time of discernment, you will want to create a healthy and supportive environment for it.

- Take some time away from your ministry environment for discernment. This may take as little as a few days or as long as a month. If you believe you don't have time to do this, *definitely* take the time to do it. You need to know that the church won't crumble without you around. If it does, all the better. It may be a sign that you need to move on because you and your church are too codependent!

- Ask people to pray for you. Whether you turn to family, girlfriends, or other ministry colleagues, surround this process with prayer. You are seeking clarity, confidence, and wisdom. You may also feel the need for healing, strength, and peace in this time. Knowing that you are not alone in this process is crucial.

- If you don't already have a relationship with a spiritual director, this would be an excellent time to speak with one. Such a person can listen and guide and help you hear the voice of God amid the noise of the anxiety, fear, and grief that this process may involve.

During your discernment process, you'll want to ask yourself the following questions:

- What are your goals for ministry? Sometimes moving from one call to the next is a career move that will advance you toward your ultimate goal. At other times, your goal may be to learn a specific set of ministry skills. Or you may be looking for a ministry context that allows you to better balance personal life and ministry. Determine what your short- and long-term goals are for ministry before you think about making a move.

- In what ways have your gifts and skills for ministry had a positive impact on the congregation you are serving? This question is important for two reasons. First, in looking for signs of life in your current call, you may discern that you don't need to leave this call after all. While frustrations and toxicity may have blinded you to the ways your ministry has been life-giving, you may find that you can work through the challenges and continue in fruitful ministry. Second, if you do discern that you are called to leave your current place of ministry, you will need to have a clear notion of how you have been effective in your ministry, so that you can articulate this insight to other churches you may interview with and apply what you have learned in your next call.

- Have you given all you have to give here? Have you really let yourself be vulnerable with this congregation? Have you done all you can to understand your ministry context and engage in it deeply? This doesn't mean you should "try harder." Sometimes it means to work smarter, not harder. If you've been running up against the same brick wall, have you checked to make sure that there isn't an opening you didn't notice because your head was aching? Have you used all the tools, all the gifts and skills you've been blessed with, to minister effectively here? Or have you been relying on those skills you are most confident in or the tools you like using the best? Be sure to explore your full range and potential before you give up on your ministry.

- Describe the perfect church for you to serve. Think about things like church size and location, but also think about the way Christian education is valued and taught. Does the congregation value intergenerational relationships and activities or is everything segregated by age and gender? Think about the mission of a church and how the congregation reaches out into the community and world. What would be the shape of a perfect staffing arrangement? While we understand that there is no such thing as the "perfect" church, it is important to dream. If, in your next call, you can serve a church that will dream the same dream you have, you may be more fulfilled and effective in your ministry.

- Have you been faithful to the "calling to which you have been called"? This is one of the questions in the Presbyterian ordination vows, and it reminds us that ministry is a two-way street. We expect God to be faithful, but we have a responsibility for faithfulness, too. Faithfulness in ministry takes many shapes. Have you faithfully served the needs of the church, or have your own needs been paramount in this ministry? Have you faithfully engaged in self-care, so that you have the energy necessary to serve in the often exhausting and emotionally draining call to pastoral ministry? Do you feel prepared for a new calling? All of these questions of faithfulness are important in the discernment process.

- What is going on in your life that colors the way you are feeling and thinking about a possible ministry transition? Examine your personal life closely during the discernment process. Like many ministry challenges, your life circumstances are subject to change. If you could see

a way through your own struggles, how might your ministry situation feel different?

* What in your life makes it possible or impossible for you
to take on a major life transition? Some women might
not be able to transition to another ministry because a
move would take their spouse away from his current job.
You may have experienced so many transitions by the
time you find your first call that it is impossible to con-
ceive of picking up and starting over again. The ties of
family and major life changes, such as having children
or financial struggles, are other factors that might in-
hibit a ministry transition. On the other hand, you may
discover, upon reflection, that the timing is ripe for this
transition in your life. Perhaps your spouse is also ready
for a career change. Or maybe this transition coincides
nicely with another life transition, such as marriage. You
may be in a situation where you don't need to sell your
home in order to move. Examine all areas of your life as
you consider what will certainly be a major life change.

* What hurtful or annoying things happened in this call
that might happen to some degree at any church you
serve? This last question might seem fairly petty, and
yet it is one of the most important questions to explore.
Ponder this question a few times over the next couple
of months and revise your list. Sometimes answers may
show up on the list because of a particularly irritating
parishioner who has taken a lot of your time recently,
but after some time has passed, you realize that this person isn't representative of the congregation as a whole.

After you feel fairly confident about your list of complaints,
call or meet with some trusted colleagues with whom you have
built strong relationships, and share your list with them. Talk
over what you have been experiencing and ask them how much
of your list overlaps with a hypothetical list they would put

together in their own situation. One of the hardest realizations in ministry is that some of our least favorite tasks or church dynamics happen everywhere. What church doesn't have at least one committee that meets forever but never gets anything done? What pastor doesn't have a parishioner who has taken it upon herself to find many ways to make your life more challenging? What pastor doesn't have moments when she feels like a congregation's mother picking up after members and reminding them when they are supposed to show up for activities?

It doesn't matter how large or small the congregation, whether you are a solo pastor, associate, or head of staff, there is always going to be some aspect of ministry that is not desirable. Some tasks in ministry—folding bulletins, coordinating building usage, and decorating bulletin boards, for example—aren't what you signed up for when you took the call, but the fact that they are far from what you learned about in seminary is of no consequence.

Moving On

We all come to terms at some point in our ministry with the fact that most of what we do isn't what we thought it would be. Wide-eyed and eager to serve God and others in worship, we will probably discover that community life and serving others on the margins can be overshadowed by discussions about the color of the carpet in the sanctuary and the financial implications of a roof with a lifetime "guarantee" that turns out not to exist. This disappointment can lead some young people to leave ministry entirely. If you are at the point of being ready to seek a new vocation, you are in good company. It may grieve you that you worked so hard through seminary, the ordination and call process, and in your ministry, only to find yourself back in the secular workforce. Take heart, girlfriend. While it saddens us that the church loses so many gifted young people, male and female, many former clergy go on to fruitful vocations in other contexts. We know bankers, woodworkers, camp directors, and professors who once served in ordained ministry and now serve God faithfully in other ways. In this difficult transition, you may find hidden gifts, discover new dimensions of your relationship with God, and unleash unknown potential.

If, in your process of discernment, you come to believe that you are being called to ordained ministry in a different place, you then have a whole new set of challenges to face. How do you look for a new call while you continue in your current ministry? How do you keep your congregation from finding out that you are searching and still draw out references from your current ministry? How do you handle the emotional roller coaster that is a natural part of this process?

There is certainly no easy way to navigate this transition, but you can make life easier on yourself. First, don't start the process until you can clearly articulate why you are leaving and what you hope to be moving to. This delay will help mitigate your feelings of guilt about leaving and keeping your search a secret. Many girlfriends have expressed that secrecy is one of the most difficult aspects of the search process, not just logistically but emotionally as well. It is hard to continue engaging in authentic ministry, leading and helping guide the vision, in a church you intend to leave in the near future. You know that your departure will likely cause the congregation grief and anxiety. But to engage fully and faithfully in your search, you must know that there is a God-given reason for your departure and a Spirit-guided search ahead of you.

Second, use whatever network of pastors you have as you begin your search. While your denomination likely has some formal procedures for searching for, or being placed in, a new call, it is always helpful to have people who know a bit about you keeping an eye out for a position that seems as if it would suit your personality, gifts, and vision. This is one of the advantages of searching for your *second* call. In seminary, most of us didn't have a network of pastors who could help us in the call process. After a few years in ministry, we have pastor friends all over the country who can let us know of openings in their areas. Use this to your advantage alongside the formal search process.

Decide whom you can trust, and keep the number small. If possible, you should have at least one person who has worked with you in your current call on your list of references. Sometimes this can be another person on staff whom you trust to keep quiet about your search. It may be a former church member who has moved elsewhere. You really want someone who will be excited about your search and encourage you in it, as well as provide a positive and accurate picture of your ministry. You may be tempted to draw several people into your search, but we recommend against it. Everyone who knows about your search will be on the emotional roller coaster with you. If these people are members of your congregation, you will have to minister to them through the ups and downs, as well as manage your own emotions. Make things easier on yourself. Keep the circle of trust tight.

Letting Go

Once you have found and accepted a new call, the final challenge will be informing your congregation. The appropriate process usually involves informing church leaders and staff, such as the head of staff, personnel committee, and church board, and allowing them to decide how to inform the congregation. Typically, this is done about a month before you intend to leave. That usually allows enough time for the congregation to absorb the shock, for you all to grieve together, for you to prepare to leave, and for the church to prepare to search for a new pastor. Some pastors tell their congregations months in advance of their departure. Others leave more abruptly. You and the leadership of your congregation will decide how much time you need.

As you pack your belongings, say good-bye to friends, and tie up as many loose ends as possible, be gentle with yourself and others. For many people, grief surfaces as anger. You may be surprised at the number of people who seem enraged by your departure. As with most things in ministry, try not to take these feelings personally, and help people move past their anger and deal with their grief, just as you would if they were mourning any other loss. During whatever "lame duck" period you have at the church, you will likely not help people move forward with ministries, visions, and new projects that you may have been engaged with. That's okay. Your most important ministry to the congregation in this time is helping the members and yourself to let go. No matter what your situation, this will likely be a sad and difficult time. Give people the space they need, and don't assume responsibility for other people's grief. Tend to your own sadness, even as you prepare for the excitement of a new adventure.

The Girlfriends' Checklist

- Make sure you've at least tried to apply tonic to a toxic situation you are in. Assess whether you've done all you can do in service to this congregation.
- Ask yourself, "Do I want to tackle the set of problems I currently face, or do I want to take on some completely unknown set of problems?"
- Take adequate time for discernment. Ask yourself difficult questions to determine how God might be working through you where you're now in ministry or where God might be calling you next.
- Consult with trusted colleagues in ministry and a spiritual director.
- Use your network of friends and ministry colleagues as you search for a new call.

- Keep the circle of trust small.
- In the departure process, be gentle with yourself and others. Tend to your grief, even as you minister to your grieving congregation.

·11·

Treading Out the Grain

REMAINING FAITHFUL TO THE CALL

Melissa Lynn DeRosia, Marianne J. Grano,
Amy Morgan, and Amanda Adams Riley

••••

The day comes for every pastor—the day when you question what you are doing. For some of us, that day is every day. It's the day when you find yourself asking, am I using my God-given talents? Am I building the church? Is what I am doing making any difference? You may wonder about other professions you might have chosen, professions that pay more money for less work, professions where no one would expect you to be perfect all the time, professions where you could actually get a good night's sleep on a Saturday night, professions where you wouldn't feel the need to take your cell phone on vacation and cancel your plans if there's a pastoral emergency.

Every minister has another profession that she could have chosen. Marianne was originally going to be an accountant. A career in accounting might sound more appealing on some days, like that day when you spent an hour in a meeting discussing how often to replace the candles on the communion table, or the day when you ran the vacuum cleaner at 7:00 a.m., because the narthex was filthy and there was going to be a funeral that morning, or the day when you asked yourself whether you needed to get a master's degree to play sardines with the youth group. For the young clergywoman, it may be the day when you hear, for the ten-thousandth time, "*You're* the pastor?" On such days you may not believe the words of 1 Timothy 3:1: "The saying is sure: whoever aspires to the office of bishop desires a noble task."

This little letter is traditionally ascribed to Paul, but whoever wrote it was a church leader, trying to bring some order into the chaotic life of the early church, which was wrenched apart from within by theological controversies, persecuted from without by the Roman authorities, abandoned by the Jewish community, disdained by the Greeks, and slandered by society as an assembly of drunkards, cannibals, and hedonists. Whatever authority asserted itself in the church was, let us say, uneven. As the early apostles began to die off or were persecuted, some communities had no leaders at all, while others were taken over by the most charismatic individual with his own interpretation of Jesus, which may or may not have been the Jesus of Scripture, given that the Bible as such didn't yet exist.

The author of 1 Timothy admonishes that such a leader cannot be a drunkard, or violent, or quarrelsome, or a lover of money—a passage that tells us that some of these leaders *were* drunkards, violent, quarrelsome, and lovers of money. Although the writer is concerned about the *episcope*, typically translated "bishop," the description really applies to any overseer or pastor. The qualifications of the pastor listed have more to do with who she is than what she does. One must be married only once, temperate, sensible, respectable, hospitable. Is the role of a pastor something to which we can aspire but never really reach? Do you really become a pastor in the moment that you are ordained or only when you reach the kingdom of heaven? The noble task of which the author speaks seems impossible. Not only must you be of perfect Christlike character, but you must lead a struggling, illegal, chaotic church at peril of your own life.

Today the ministry may be legal, but ministers no longer command the respect of society as they once did. With a church that is slowly aging and losing members and money, still beset by controversies and infighting, this is one of the most difficult times in history to be a pastor and not unlike the days of the early church. It's a tiring, draining, and often unappreciated task. No wonder more than 50 percent of ordained ministers drop out of professional ministry in the first ten years.

There's an image for ministry the author of 1 Timothy uses in chapter 5, an image drawn from Paul's first letter to the Corinthians, which in turn draws from Deuteronomy 25:4: "You shall not muzzle an ox while it is treading out the grain." Paul talks about the minister as a brute ox, treading over and over the same path, stomping and plodding forward, step after step. Oxen were used to tread the grain on the threshing floor and separate the wheat from the chaff. They were yoked together and whipped as they did this work. This image of ministry is a dirty, earthy one. But Paul ministered in dirty, earthy places—in houses and marketplaces, on boats, and in jail. Paul was whipped, beaten, and exhausted for the sake of this noble task. The ox, plodding ever forward, carrying his heavy yoke, reminds us of Paul but also reminds us of God entering fully into our dirty, earthy life, of Jesus ministering to the crowds when he was tired and in need of refreshment, of Jesus carrying our burden ever forward, plodding on, of Jesus doing his ministry on the cross.

The minister is not the proud lion, king of everything he surveys. Not the wise owl, with surpassing knowledge and insight. Not the noble eagle flying overhead, able to see everything clearly. The minister is a big, plodding ox doing tiring, draining, unappreciated physical labor—such as running the vacuum cleaner in the narthex at 7:00 a.m. But do you realize what the ox is doing as he plods forward, carrying that heavy burden, endlessly treading, one hoof after the other? The ox is making something people need. The ox is creating the bread of life.

From the moment you were called to ministry, you've been hooked up to this yoke—and you've been making the bread of life for people. When you study the Scriptures and write another sermon, you're treading out the grain that will feed people for that week. When you sit in a meeting about trash bags, you're milling the flour that will help someone know Christian fellowship. When you play sardines with the youth group, you're kneading the dough that will rise in a young person's life. When you hold a hand in a hospital bed, you're filling someone with the spiritual nourishment of God's presence. And each time you say those familiar words on Sunday morning, and you lift that bread and cup in the presence of the whole congregation, you are giving people what they most need—the very bread of life.

You could not have been an accountant.

Like Jesus, like Paul, like the ox, you never really had a choice. You did not choose the ministry. The ministry chose you. People who choose to go into ministry find that they no longer feel that spiritual fire. When the ministry chooses you, however, you grow so much closer to God that others are comforted by your very presence. People who choose to go into ministry find themselves becoming quarrelsome, or drunkards, or lovers of money. When the ministry chooses you, you become more Christlike, more temperate, sensible, respectable, and hospitable, and in time you become more and more of an apt teacher. People who choose to go into ministry see only the numbers on the budget sheet and the attendance rolls. When the ministry chooses you, you are always seeing signs of God's miracles around you. People who choose to go into ministry drop out in a year or two. When the ministry chooses you, you may never really retire. People who choose to go into ministry become bitter and angry with the church. When the ministry chooses you, at the very moment that you're ready to give up, someone approaches you and tells you how you have affected his life. People who choose to go into ministry become exhausted and drained and won't take another plodding step. When the ministry chooses you, you find that you are making the bread of life.

The Bible says, in three places, that you should not muzzle the ox while it is treading out the grain. The muzzle won't let the ox eat any of the grain, but the ox needs grain too. The pastor needs to eat too—to take in spiritual, emotional, and financial nourishment. Take time every day to thank God for the blessings you have received. Make sure you are getting your time off, you are getting timely raises, you are getting the grain you need. If you make sure that you are well nourished, you will find that you can nourish others. You will find that you can remain faithful to this call. You will find that this is truly a noble and rewarding task.

Where We Are Treading Out the Grain Today

Since we began this project several years ago, God's voice took each of the four of us in a new direction, but we still keep treading grain, making the bread of life in communities of faith. Through this book, you have come to know us and our stories, so we thought you might be interested in and encouraged by God's continued faithfulness to us, even as our sense of God's call changes. Here's what treading out the grain looks like for each of us today.

Marianne

These days I feel as though I'm treading out the grain twenty-four hours a day. No one ever told me it would be this hard. At 2:00 a.m., my day begins with the baby screaming. I wake up, hold the baby, rock the baby. Then at 5:00 a.m., again, the screaming. I feed the baby, hold the baby, rock the baby. Then at 7:00 a.m., I feed the baby, change the baby, dress the baby, make the coffee, make the breakfast, take a shower while the baby screams, carry the baby plus eight bags to the freezing car. Then I drop off the baby at the babysitter's house, drive to work, do paperwork, go to meetings, write a sermon, try to shed some light into the darkness of life. Then I drive back to the babysitter's house, pick up the baby, feed the baby, change the baby, hold the baby, rock the baby, put the baby to bed, do the dishes, and fall asleep on the couch at 8:30. My husband wakes me up at 10:00 to go to bed. And at 2:00 a.m., again I hear the screaming. It's a never-ending struggle just to get through one more day, only to find another day staring at me, with endless work, endless struggle, and endless tasks screaming to be completed.

I am being honest only because I hope that other women considering ministry and motherhood have a realistic idea of what it can be like. I have a great respect today for full-time mothers and fathers, and I understand why so many women leave full-time ministry when they have children—and why those who remain often have only one child. Ministry and motherhood are alike in that both are jobs that never really end. You're never off the clock.

Thank God that God is never off the clock either. God has placed people in my life and in my church who have been willing to take on more because I can do less. God has given me reminders of my calling. God has shown me how I am making the bread of life in my church. Taking the time and energy to eat some of that bread, to take in spiritual, emotional, and physical nourishment, has become less possible and more necessary since I became a mother. I pray while I'm nursing, and I take my moments of calm when I can get them.

I wonder if I'm doing a 50 percent job as a pastor and a 50 percent job as a mom; then I trust God to do what I can't.

I wonder about another call or another kid; then I trust God to show me when the time is right. I wonder whether I can get through this day, this week, or this year; then I trust the God who's gotten me this far to bring me through. In the words of the black church tradition, "He never failed me yet"—and I don't expect him to start now.

Melissa

For the most part, my babies have stopped screaming. They've gotten older, and the whining is at least in complete sentences. With those complete sentences comes the inevitable question that pastors' kids ask: "Do you have to go to another meeting?" For the first few years of their lives, the calls of ministry and motherhood were intrinsically woven together with little or no separation. As I began listening to the ways God was calling me in ministry, it was clear that for me to be a faithful pastor and an "as good as I can be" mom, I needed more separation between the two callings. The kids started in full-time day care, and I entered into a time of listening with God and asking myself a lot of the questions we discussed in chapter 10.

The context in which I was serving was not entirely toxic. It was filled with people whom I loved and who felt passionately about the church they and their families had worshiped in for generations. But there were many times when I left meetings or worship scratching my head and wondering what it was this community of faith believed God was calling its members to do and be. Together the congregation and I entered into two separate discernment processes—times of praying, asking questions, and listening to one another reflect on what God was calling this congregation to do and be in the world today. It became evident that the mission and ministry to which the people felt God calling them did not match the ways in which God was calling me to use my gifts and skills, and I began the process of searching for a new call as a solo pastor or head of staff.

The search process itself is one of plodding and not being able to see how the grain will eventually become the bread. The string of rejection letters can feel like lashes striking an already tender and vulnerable skin, but one step at a time I kept moving, believing that for God and me to remain faithful to this journey of "call," I had to be patient. Still, I was hoping that God would honor my patience and move a little bit faster.

At this point it would be nice to offer some sort of cliché like "patience paid off" or "it happened in God's time." Even though God and I ended this leg of the search journey in an amazing place, I still find all those clichés to be annoying and try not to downplay how hard the search process can be for those in the thick of it. The truth is, God was smack-dab in the middle of what ended up being a two-year search for a call to serve a community of faith that needed my gifts and skills and was willing to look beyond stereotypes of what the pastor "should" look like, to find a pastor who fit the work members felt God was calling them to. I had heard rumors that such congregations existed, but I wasn't so sure.

I am still brushing the shards of glass from my hair after bursting through the "stained-glass ceiling." Now as I serve as the pastor and head of staff of a six-hundred-member congregation with another female clergy on staff, "treading out the grain" in ministry has a familiar feel but one requiring a new and challenging skill set. I have gone from "flying solo" to being airborne with a staff team engaged in collaborative ministry. Right now, I am taking one day at a time and putting one foot in front of the other.

Amy

Toward the beginning of my third year in ministry, after going through a number of difficult situations personally and professionally, I had lunch with a congregation member who is also a licensed counselor. She told me that my faith had talons. I realized that that was exactly the way I had felt since I graduated from seminary. Through living in my parents' basement with a new baby, moving to Michigan in the middle of January, my husband's long and arduous job search, a sanctuary renovation and an interim head of staff, staff layoffs and budget cuts, a miscarriage, anxiety, and loneliness, I felt that God was gripping me by the shoulders with strong talons, holding me up and helping me soar even in the midst of all the challenges, transitions, and pains. I didn't have a strong faith in God. God had a strong faith in me. That's what kept me treading out the grain.

When I told this congregation member how strongly I connected to that image, she told me, "Yes, but hope is the thing with feathers." She was a quoting from an Emily Dickinson poem, and she later gave me a pocket collection of Dickinson's poems, so that I could keep that thought with me.

The following years proved her right once again. As a new head of staff arrived, the financial condition of the church stabilized, the loan for the sanctuary renovation got paid off, my husband landed his dream job, my son grew and gained independence, and we purchased our dream home just a block from the church. Hope fluttered in my soul. Hope kept me treading out the grain.

The apostle Paul talks about faith and hope, and finally love. And, Paul says, "now faith, hope, and love abide, these three; and the greatest of these is love" (1 Cor. 13:13). I began to wonder if, after all that I had been through, I could really come to love this place and these people. Of course, a pastor *should* love the people in her congregation. She should love everyone. That's what Jesus did and taught. But in my first years in ministry, it was difficult to love anyone or anything. Once I knew God was calling me into deeper relationship with my congregation, however, once I realized how God might work through me and even transform my own life, once I began to see how God was making bread in this place, hope slowly began singing a love song.

Don't get me wrong: I still have my moments. I recently had to buy a pair of cowboy boots to boost my self-confidence after a particularly defeating committee meeting, and there are days when waitressing still sounds romantic. However, I now know I love the people, place, and position God has called me to, and while I'm trying to remain open to what God may call me to next, I'm also hoping it will involve walking to my son's football games at the high school down the street. This place is fertile soil.

Amanda

Coming off a summer of treading out the grain through four youth trips, which are both part of the constant plodding of ministry and among the ministries I find nourishing and life-giving, I entered into an unintentional sabbatical. On Saturday, I returned home from a youth conference, Sunday morning was my last Sunday as associate pastor of the First Presbyterian Church of Fenton, and Monday morning a moving truck pulled up in front of my house.

Earlier in the summer, after much discussion and prayerful deliberation, my husband had accepted a position in the aerospace industry in Los Angeles. This meant that I would move three thousand miles away without a call, trusting that God, who is faithful, would provide—and she has.

After spending three months learning what I could about church life on the West Coast and enjoying an unplanned sabbatical, I took a part-time parish associate position. Today, treading out the grain looks quite different from full-time ministry for me. I still have night meetings, and I am doing some program work—but I don't feel the same about time. When I was serving full-time, I felt that every minute mattered. If I wasn't on church time, then I was on "family time" or "personal time" or "my day off." I now have the luxury of taking however long it takes to answer e-mails or prepare to lead worship. Hospital and home visitation no longer feels like a time sink on my to-do list, something I have to make time for to do right. Now I have the luxury of sitting, listening, and praying with members for however long is needed, and I feel free to journey with them without the pressure of a program-heavy to-do list.

Part of treading out the grain is patience. As a summer camp counselor, I lost track of the number of times I was told, "You are sowing seeds." Today I am waiting to see what seeds have been sown in me and what the springtime growth will yield. Looking toward our cross-country move, I would have been happy to walk into another full-time position, but that was not the plan. So I wait, I pray, and I look forward to discovering where and to what God is calling me next.

A Prayer for Our Girlfriends

God of our Lives,
thank you for calling young women throughout time
to lead, to minister, to serve.
Bless those who take up your yoke today,
who tread out the grain—
in the pulpit and the pantry,
in the emergency room and the youth room,
at the graveside and in the garden.
For all the ways you choose us,
for the different ways you use us,
we are grateful to know whose you made us to be.
Amen.

Notes

CHAPTER 1: THE DATING GAME

1. In the United States, churches are employers and are therefore subject to employment laws issued by the U.S. Department of Labor. There are surprisingly few exceptions to these laws for religious organizations.

2. There are several good cost-of-living calculators online, such as the one on Bankrate.com.

CHAPTER 2: FLYING SOLO

1. Mark Lau Branson, *Memories, Hopes, and Conversations: Appreciative Inquiry and Congregational Change* (Herndon, VA: Alban Institute, 2004).

CHAPTER 4: PASTORS ON PARADE

1. Kenda Creasy Dean and Ron Foster, *The Godbearing Life: The Art of Soul Tending for Youth Ministry* (Nashville: Upper Room Books, 1998), 48.

2. Rosemary Radford Ruether, *Sexism and God-Talk: Toward a Feminist Theology* (Boston: Beacon Press, 1993), 72–79.

3. Frank A. Thomas, *They Like to Never Quit Praisin' God: The Role of Celebration in Preaching* (Cleveland: Pilgrim Press, 1997), 12.

4. George Herbert, "The Collar" (1633), Christian Classics Ethereal Library, accessed March 29, 2011, http://www.ccel.org/h/herbert/temple/Collar.html.

Chapter 8: You May Be a Master of Divinity: But You Are Not Superwoman

1. *John Mark Ministries*, "Ex-Pastors," http://jmm.aaa.net.au/articles/21074.htm.

Chapter 9: Tiresome, Taxing, and Toxic

1. Sheryl Crow, Bill Bottrell, Kevin Gilbert, and Dan Schwartz. "No One Said It Would Be Easy." *Tuesday Night Music Club*. A&M Records, 1993.

2. Family systems theory is the concept that family relationships and interactions can be treated as a system that affects all other relationships and interactions. For more information on family systems theory, see the website www.thebowencenter.org. See also Edwin H. Friedman, *Generation to Generation: Family Process in Church and Synagogue* (New York: Guilford Press, 1985); and Peter L. Steinke, *How Your Church Family Works: Understanding Congregations as Emotional Systems* (Herndon, VA: Alban Institute, 1985).

Contributors

The Rev. Melissa DeRosia is the pastor and head of staff at Gates Presbyterian Church in Rochester, New York. She is a graduate from Alma College and Louisville Presbyterian Theological Seminary where she was the recipient of the George and Jean Edwards Award in the Interpretation of Scripture and Christian Life. Passionate and dedicated to follow God's call in the changing landscape of the church, she served as Moderator of the Presbytery of Lake Huron and is an elected member of the PC (USA) General Assembly Mission Council.

The Rev. Marianne J. Grano is a graduate of the University of Michigan and McCormick Theological Seminary and currently serves as associate pastor and director of youth ministries at University Presbyterian Church in Rochester Hills, Michigan. She was the keynote speaker for the 2011 Alma Youth Mix of the Presbyteries of Lake Huron and Lake Michigan, and shares her sermons and spiritual reflections through www.thesermonator.blogspot.com.

The Rev. Amy Morgan holds a Bachelor of Fine Arts degree from New York University and a Master of Divinity from Princeton Theological Seminary where she served as comoderator of the Women's Center. She has been an actress, waitress, barista, teacher, wife, mother, and pastor. She currently serves as associate pastor and director of youth ministries at First Presbyterian Church of Birmingham, Michigan and is an active member of Detroit Presbytery's Youth Council.

The Rev. Amanda Adams Riley is a graduate of Princeton Theological Seminary and James Madison University. Amanda has served as a resident in parish ministry in Ann Arbor, Michigan and as associate pastor in Fenton, MI. While in Lake Huron Presbytery, she served as vice moderator of the Committee on Ministry. Amanda is currently enrolled in the Doctor of Ministry Program at McCormick Theological Seminary, and serves as a parish associate at Brentwood Presbyterian Church in Los Angeles, California.